Uniform with this Volume:

JANE AUSTEN *by Margaret Kennedy*
THE BRONTËS *by Phyllis Bentley*
D H LAWRENCE *by Anthony West*

THE EUROPEAN NO

HENRY FIE

HENRY FIELDING

ELIZABETH JENKINS

ARTHUR BARKER LIMITED
20 NEW BOND STREET LONDON W I

Printed in Great Britain by
Lowe & Brydone (Printers) Ltd., London

HENRY FIELDING

THE rise and flowering of the English novel as a great work of imagination has been rapid and short-lived. The form was unknown at the beginning of the eighteenth century, yet the middle of the century saw the publication of *Clarissa* (1748), *Tom Jones* (1749) and *Tristram Shandy* (1760). The art was practised with consummate brilliance during the early and middle years of the nineteenth century, and most people would agree that the period of genius was over with the death of Dickens in 1870.

What has happened is plain enough. It is the decay of imagination. *Why* it has happened is the subject of long and inconclusive arguments, but certain facts have an inescapable significance. The era of Fielding's life (he died in 1754) was marked by horrors in the daily life of large numbers of the population, such as we cannot read of without a shudder ; Johnson computed that one thousand people starved to death in London alone every year ; the state of prisons was such that whatever crime the prisoner had committed against society it could not equal the crime of which society was guilty against him ; the exquisite song in *The Beggar's Opera*, comparing an innocent girl who becomes a whore to a flower that, cast aside, " rots, stinks and dies and is trod underfeet," was no allegory to an eighteenth-century audience, but a plain statement of fact. Nor were the fortunate classes immune ; they endured operations without anæsthetics, illnesses without drugs, and so widespread was the desolation of maternal

and infant mortality, that Gibbon thought himself fortunate,
sickly child as he was, to have survived, since, he said,
"not one male child in ten lives to see the age of
twenty-one."

But fearful as these conditions were, they were not those
which prevent the bringing forth of great works of art ;
further, they were accompanied by conditions which were
favourable to the growth of the imagination, such as the small-
ness of the population, the fact that man still had to do many
things for himself which are now done by machinery, and
that, for those who had sufficient food, the food was of
excellent quality. It has been considered a possible factor
in the decline of population in our own day, that most of
our food has ceased to be home-grown. If this be true, it
seems reasonable to suggest that what affects the fertility
of man's body, will also affect the fertility of man's mind ;
and if so, it is interesting to compare the eggs and sugar,
the cream and wine, that went to make the eighteenth-century
syllabub, with the frozen custard-powder mixture, the syn-
thetic cream and the dab of fruit-extract flavoured jam which
compose its modern counterpart, the " sundae."

The difference between the population of England in
the eighteenth century and the twentieth, however, is a
factor of self-evident importance, beyond which we need
not go, when we ask ourselves the reason for the decline
of literature, architecture, design and craftsmanship. The
population of England and Wales in 1750 was just over six
million. The population of London in the middle of the
eighteenth century was about two hundred and fifty thousand.
The present population figures are enough to account for most
of the decline in our imaginative faculties. Size, congestion
and mass production create conditions, which, however

excellent in matters of hygiene and social welfare generally, are the doom of man's imagination. Life, by becoming increasingly mechanical, becomes less conscious.

We are surprised at the intensity of emotion displayed even by our Victorian ancestors, their anger and their loyalty, their passionate grief at bereavement, their religious fervour and their family affection. Our own emotions seem transitory and faint beside what we read of theirs. To-day we have a large measure of social justice, good drains, chloroform, cleanliness, unemployment insurance, effective spectacles and false teeth. Our ancestors in the eighteenth century had none of these things ; but they had æsthetic genius and the powerful imagination which is its motive force.

If we regard at all the misery of large numbers of our fellow-creatures, we cannot regret the passing of the eighteenth and early nineteenth centuries, but while we think over what we have gained, the more thoughtful of us are sometimes chilled to remember what we have lost. That is why, apart from the sheer pleasure they were created to give, the great novels of the past are so precious to us now. Like the music, the painting, the poetry, of the great eras of imagination, they give us something that we cannot any longer make for ourselves. They renew the spirit of man.

Henry Fielding was born at Sharpham Park in Somerset in 1707. The house belonged to his grandfather, Sir Henry Gould, a judge of the King's Bench. His mother came here for the birth of her first child as her husband, the Hon. Edmund Fielding, was a lieutenant in Marlborough's army and on active service at the time.

Lieutenant, afterwards General Fielding, was a handsome,

good-natured man, a fine soldier but unreliable in private life. His parents-in-law, who had never much liked the match for their daughter, presently became openly hostile to him. When Sir Henry Gould died in 1710, he left an estate worth £3000 for the benefit of his daughter and her children, her husband, the will expressly stated, to have " nothing to do with it." Mrs. Fielding had six surviving children, two sons and four daughters. She died in 1718, when the eldest, Henry, was eleven.

The following year, General Fielding married again. To the dismay of the children's grandmother, he married a woman called Eleanor Rasa, a Roman Catholic and the widow of an Italian, who kept a London eating-house. The second Mrs. Fielding at once began to raise a second family. Meanwhile, the first family of children were shipped off to boarding-school and Lady Gould took a house in Salisbury so as to be near the little girls.

By 1721, the unscrupulous, happy-go-lucky General Fielding had involved himself in a serious quarrel with his mother-in-law. Old Lady Gould was not the widow of a judge for nothing. In this year she filed a Bill of Complaint in the Court of Chancery, in the name of Henry Fielding and his brother and sisters, stating that the income from the estate inherited from their mother was being diverted by their father to his own use. In the course of this action many aspects of the family quarrel came to light. Henry had run away from Eton and presented himself at his grandmother's house, not, presumably, because he was unhappy at school, but simply for a lark and to show on whose side of the quarrel he was. He was said also to have " carried himself very unhandsomely " towards his step-mother. Lady Gould had been driven nearly frantic by hearing that

General Fielding had said he approved of the bringing up of young persons in monasteries. The bitter quarrel, personal, financial and religious, was decided in Lady Gould's favour on every point. The charge was proved against General Fielding, the children were to stay at their present schools, and Henry was to spend his holidays at his grandmother's house.

Henry was a handsome, high-spirited boy with black eyes and a grecian nose. From the way he afterwards wrote of it, he appears to have enjoyed himself at Eton. He said he was often flogged, but he did not criticise the way in which he was taught. He came away " uncommonly versed in the Greek and Latin authors." The foundation of that learning, which, so easily carried, is so marked a feature of his style, was laid at school. Fielding's was not learning for its own sake, the precocious pedantry of a clever boy. His learning is intelligible to the unlearned reader because it is conveyed in the form of a philosophy of life, which everyone can understand even if he cannot apply it for himself. Speaking of the works of Aristotle and Plato, " with the rest of those inestimable treasures which ancient Greece had bequeathed to the world," Fielding says : " They elevate the mind and steel and harden it against the capricious invasions of fortune " (*Tom Jones*, Bk. VIII, Chap. XIII) ; and it was told of him that under the load of illness, poverty and distress he would be discovered quietly reading to himself Cicero's *De Consolatione*.

At the age of nineteen he makes a brief appearance at Lyme, attempting to run off with a beautiful heiress, who was herself by no means unwilling, and her guardian complained to the magistrates that he went in fear of personal violence " from Henry Fielding and his man." Fielding, in his

youth, was not only handsome and overflowing with vitality
and animal spirits ; he was also uncommonly susceptible.
His writings show that he was one of those men who have
an immense enthusiasm for women. Some of the most
exquisite feelings of his nature were called out by this, and
the same susceptibility, particularly in what he calls " my
boyish years," naturally drove him into a wild and even
sordid phase of existence. Twenty-five years afterwards,
he gives a backward glance at some of the experiences of his
early life :

> " I happened in my youth to sit behind two ladies in a side
> box at a play, where, in the balcony on the opposite side was
> placed the inimitable B(ets)y C(areles)s [1] in company with a
> young fellow of no very formal or indeed sober appearance.
> One of the ladies, I remember, said to the other : Did you
> ever see anything look so modest and so innocent as that girl
> over the way ? What a pity it is such a creature should be in
> the way of ruin, as I am afraid she is, by her being alone with
> that young fellow ! Now this lady was no bad physiognomist ;
> for it was impossible to conceive a greater appearance of
> modesty, innocence and simplicity than what nature had dis-
> displayed in the countenance of that girl ; and yet, all appear-
> ances notwithstanding, I myself (remember, critics, it was in
> my youth) had a few mornings before, seen that very identical
> picture of all those engaging qualities in bed with a rake at a
> bagnio, smoking tobacco, drinking punch, talking obscenity,
> and swearing and cursing with all the impudence and impiety
> of the lowest and most abandoned trull of a soldier." (*Amelia*,
> Bk. I, Chap. VI.)

At nineteen, Fielding was living as his own master in
London. The quarrel with his father was long since worn
out. His son always spoke of him kindly. General Fielding,
anxious, like Sir Anthony Absolute, to see his boy cut some

---

[1] Betsy Careless in middle age is represented in the mysterious Plate III of
Marriage à la Mode. She is the woman opening a penknife, and has " E.C."
tattooed in gunpowder on her bosom.

figure in the world, had promised him an allowance of
£200 a year, but, as Fielding said afterwards, anyone might
pay the money who would. His father's country house
was open to him when he could not get a dinner or a bed in
London. For the next ten years, he probably owed a good
deal to the generosity of his friends ; in so far as he maintained himself, he did it by play-writing.

This period of his life brought him into touch with the
actor, Arthur Murphy (Dr. Johnson's friend, whom he
called " Mur "). Eight years after Fielding's death, Murphy
brought out an edition of his works, to which he added a
biographical preface. In the dearth of first-hand information
about Fielding, this essay by a man who knew him is of
unique value. It has been proved very inaccurate in matters
of fact, but it gives passages of description which are the
only available material of their kind. Murphy bears tribute
to the extraordinary strength both of mind and body, the
physical vitality and the wonderful charm compounded of a
powerful intellect and a generous, emotional nature. He
speaks of " the brilliancy of his wit, the vivacity of his
humour, and his high relish of social enjoyment." Fielding,
Murphy says, was never daunted by difficulties. His temper
was quick and when angry he spoke harshly, but he was
without a trace of vindictiveness. " From his silence you
had nothing to fear." He was above six feet tall, large
built and remarkably robust. Frequently in his novels he
displays an artless contempt for men of feeble physique
when they take it upon themselves to show off in front of
women. In *Joseph Andrews*, when the hero has carried
Fanny down the bank in his arms, Fielding warns young
ladies how they trust themselves to a spindle-shanked beau
who would, in an emergency, be more likely to need help

than to give it, and in *Amelia*, when the lovers, eloping
but not yet married, decline the offer of the old cottage-
woman's bed, he makes Captain Booth say that, as the old
lady supposed them to be married, this hesitation on his
part should have filled her with " the utmost contempt "
for him.

With this tremendous zest for life, coupled, as it very
seldom is, with unusual powers of eye and ear, and with
the beginnings of literary genius, Fielding was equipped for
writing for the stage, and made his livelihood, precarious
though it was, by doing so from 1727 to 1737.

A distant cousin by his father's side was the Lady Mary
Wortley Montagu, older than himself and established in the
fashionable world ; Fielding showed her his first play and
Lady Mary read it, praised it and attended one of the per-
formances. The gratitude with which Fielding records
this condescension on her part reads oddly now, but in the
restricted social sphere of 1727, Lady Mary's suffrages had
their use. Fielding's real indebtedness, however, was to
the actress Mrs. Oldfield. This mature but still fascinating
star had just finished the phenomenal run of *The Provok'd
Husband*, in which she played Lady Townley. She was kind
to the handsome young author, and she thought his play
good enough to follow *The Provok'd Husband*.

Love in Several Masques was put on at Drury Lane in 1728,
and was a gratifying success. The somewhat stilted intrigue
is woven between three sets of lovers, in the manner of
Congreve and Wycherley without Congreve's enchanting
brilliance or Wycherley's brute force. Nevertheless, the
character-drawing is interesting. Mrs. Oldfield played Lady
Matchless, the rich and lovely widow who is converted from
the emptiness of fashionable society by the country gentle-

man, Mr. Wisemore.   Her niece Helena is an unusually vivid
sketch of a tart and saucy girl.   The best character is that of
Sir Positive Trap, so besotted with family pride that he
believes Julius Cæsar to have been a Trap by the mother's
side.   There is also a good part of a town fop, Rattle.   This
was played by Colley Cibber.

There were at this time four theatres in town :   the Opera
House in the Haymarket, the Little or New Theatre, almost
opposite, a theatre in Lincoln's Inn Fields (where *The Beggar's
Opera* was brought out, and was running at the time *Love
in Several Masques* was produced) and the Theatre Royal,
Drury Lane.   This was managed by Colley Cibber, and his
partners, the actors Booth and Wilkes.

Fielding did not immediately follow up his theatrical
success.   He appears in the same year registered as a law
student in the University of Leyden.   But in less than two
years he was in London again, possibly because his father
was not able to continue to pay his fees ;   and now, in his
own words, he had to choose between becoming a hackney
writer or a hackney coachman.   In 1730 his second play,
The Temple Beau, another comedy on the model of the
" wit-traps " of Congreve, was produced at the newly
opened theatre in Goodman's Fields, and he had settled to an
existence of gaiety and extravagance, alternating with the
shifts and humiliations of poverty.   In the small orbit of
eighteenth-century London, where " Society " was reckoned
to consist of twelve hundred persons, he was, if not very
successful, at least very well known, and a writer in *The
Gentleman's Magazine* describes him as wearing now a
frieze coat, now a laced one :

> For last night lay
> In pawn the velvet which he wears to-day.

Fielding said in after years that he left off writing for the stage at the point where he ought to have begun, and Murphy, who as an actor could speak on this part of Fielding's life, at least, with authority, said : " Generally his judgement was very little consulted, and indeed how could it be otherwise ? When he had contracted to bring on a play or a farce . . . he would go home rather late from a tavern, and would, the next morning, deliver a scene to the players, written upon the papers which had wrapped the tobacco in which he so much delighted."

He wrote more than twenty plays and farces, and after the two first, he entered on and developed a vein of his own. The best part of Fielding's work is not found among his dramatic pieces, but these show a power of vivid, immediate characterisation, a great sense of humour, and an unusual capacity for reflecting the topical scene. To anyone who is looking at the work of eighteenth-century dramatists as an illustration of contemporary life, Fielding's plays offer a much wider field than those of any other eighteenth-century dramatist before Sheridan.

Among the most notable is *The Author's Farce*, produced in 1730. This contains a description of the author (Luckless) which so exactly bears out what Murphy, Lady Mary Wortley Montagu and the critic of *The Gentleman's Magazine* said about Fielding himself, one cannot but think of it as a piece of autobiography. The landlady exclaims : " Never tell me Mr. Luckless, of your play and your play. I tell you I must be paid. I would no more depend on a benefit night of an unacted play than I would on a benefit ticket of an undrawn lottery. Could I have guessed that I had a poet in my house ! Could I have looked for a poet under laced clothes ? . . . I'm resolved when you have gone away (which I heartily hope will be very soon), I'll hang over my door in great red letters, ' No lodgings for poets.' There never was such a guest as you have been. My floor is all spoiled with ink, my windows with verses, and my door has been almost beat down with duns." Again she says : " You have been a nuisance to the whole neighbourhood. While you had money, my doors were thundered at every morning at four and five, by coachmen and chairmen ; and since you have had none, my house has been besieged all day by creditors and bailiffs."

In the same year, Fielding produced, for the first time, and though still using the form of farce, one of those vitriolic comments on an abuse of the times which cause him to be regarded as the great precursor of Dickens. In *Rape upon Rape, or, The Justice Caught in His Own Trap*, he gives, in Justice Squeezum, the first of those portraits which made Thackeray say that Fielding had an eye that brightened up a rogue like a constable's lantern. Justice Squeezum makes his first appearance with his clerk Quill :

> SQUEEZUM. Did Mother Bilkum refuse to pay my demands, say you ?
>
> QUILL. Yes sir, she says she does not value your Worship's protection a farthing. For that, she can bribe two juries a year to acquit her in Hick's Hall, for half the money which she hath paid you within these three months.
>
> SQUEEZUM. Very fine ! I'll show her that I understand something of juries as well as herself. Quill, make a memorandum against Mother Bilkum's trial, that we may remember to have the panel No. 3. They are a set of good men and true, and hearken to no evidence but mine.

The plot, though extremely sordid, is replete with humour ; as when Ramble and his friend Constant are severally taken up for rape which neither has committed, and Constant being established in a private room, the constable Staff, wants to lock up Ramble with him, saying :

> STAFF. I have but this one prison room, Captain, besides I assure you, this is no common fellow, but a very fine gentleman, a captain too—and as merry a one——
>
> CONSTANT. What is the cause of his misfortune ?
>
> STAFF. A rape, Captain, a rape—no dishonourable offence—I would not have brought any scoundrel into your honour's company, but rape and murder no gentleman need be ashamed of, and this is an honest brother ravisher.

1730 was a prolific year with Fielding, for in it he also produced the most successful farce he ever wrote and one of the most successful, in its own time, ever produced— this was *The Tragedy of Tragedies, or, The Life and Death of Tom Thumb the Great*. As a burlesque of the grandiose and lifeless tragedies of the times the title alone is a masterpiece. The course of time which has obliterated the tragedies of Thomson and Lee has of course diminished the success of their parody, but much of *Tom Thumb* is admirable reading still, and so are the " notes " with which Fielding supplied the published version of the play in imitation of the contemporary critics. For example :

> " The mighty Thomas Thumb victorious comes

Note : Dr. B——y reads : The mighty tall-mast Thumb. Mr. D——s : The mighty Thumbing Thumb. Mr. T——d reads : Thundering. I think Thomas more agreeable to the great simplicity so apparent in our author."

Swift told Laetitia Pilkington that he had been made to laugh only twice in his life, once at a Merry-Andrew and once at a performance of *Tom Thumb*. The farce was acted on and off during the next hundred years.[1] From the

[1] Fanny Burney gives a delightful account of its performance in her family, with her little cousin taking the part of Tom Thumb.

financial standpoint, however, Fielding had a greater success with two adaptations from Molière, *The Mock Doctor* and *The Miser*. These were not only a theatrical success but Voltaire said the translator had added beauties of his own.

By 1733, Fielding was involved in a theatrical quarrel which has become historical, although its origins remain unknown. Colley. Cibber's *Apology*, which he published in 1738, is so fascinating as a history of the stage from 1660 onwards, that the modern reader cannot but be very much influenced in his favour by it. His descriptions of acting, notably of Betterton's and Mrs. Mountford's, are with Hazlitt's and Lamb's the finest things of their kind ever written. In his own account of his managerial career, he appears as a shrewd, sensible, tactful business man and a sound, disarmingly modest actor. His appointment as Poet Laureate was no doubt absurd, but, even so, he seems scarcely worth that bad eminence which he occupies in the *Dunciad*. Anyone, however, might have had the misfortune to irritate Pope, but to have got thoroughly across Fielding suggests that the fault was, to say the least of it, on both sides.

Cibber sold his shares in Drury Lane to a new management, and when the sale was completed and could not be injured, his son Theophilus and several others of the company left the theatre in a body. But inconvenienced as they were, the new management was saved by the fact that they retained the biggest box-office draw of the whole ; this was the quick-tempered but loyal Mrs. Clive, now twenty-three years old, and just beginning that career which for fifty years she maintained as the greatest comic actress on the English stage.

" Clive," said Dr. Johnson, " is a good thing to sit by.

2

She always understands what you say," and he added that she was the best player he ever saw. Hogarth's portrait shows that her large-featured, angular face was not beautiful but irradiated with a barely suppressed gleefulness. When Garrick was her manager, Drury Lane rang to her tremendous disputes with him, and it was said that she drove him about the theatre like a terrier after a rat, but unreasonable as she might be, she had a fierce love of justice and fair play. She had acted in several of Fielding's plays, and for the new management he adapted for her Regnard's *Le Retour Imprévu,* and made it a star-vehicle, called *The Intriguing Chambermaid.* His dedication to Mrs. Clive of the published play calls her not only the finest of comic actresses, but the best daughter and wife and friend in the world. At the same time was put on a revised edition of *The Author's Farce,* into which Fielding had written a little recognition of the Cibbers, father and son, as the Marplays.

> MARPLAY JUNIOR. Yes, sir, alterations—I will maintain it. Let a play be never so good, without alterations it will do nothing. . . . When you write yourself, you will find the necessity of alterations—Why sir, would you guess that I had altered *Shakespeare* ?
> WITMORE. Yes, faith, sir, no one sooner.
> MARPLAY JUNIOR. . . . The poet make the play, indeed ! The colourman might be as well said to make the picture or the weaver the coat. My father and I, sir, are a couple of poetical tailors ; when a play is brought us, we consider it as a tailor does his coat, we cut it, sir, we cut it.

Don Quixote, produced in 1734, is interesting, for it is the first expression of Fielding's admiration for Cervantes, who was to be so important an influence on him as a novelist. The imitation of the character is a very intelligent one, for after behaving as a complete absurdity till almost the end, Don Quixote then makes some observations on forced marriages, perfectly in the shrewd, gentle, highminded manner of the great original, and altogether putting to shame the supposedly sane persons of the play. Further, the piece contains a brief but blistering satire on the corruptness of elections, a theme which Fielding was to exploit further, with momentous consequences. He said that the draft of *Don Quixote* had been made while he was at Leyden ; possibly to this early period belong the two songs in it : " The Roast Beef of Old England," which was taken up all over the house when the audience objected to a company of French actors being brought on to the stage, and the one and only poetic verse which, so far as we know, Fielding ever wrote, the hunting song beginning :

The dusky night rides down the sky.

In 1735, another play was written specially for Mrs. Clive : *The Virgin Unmasked,* an enchanting little farce which gave her, in " Lucy," one of those romping parts of a tomboy with the ignorant shrewdness of a changeling, in which she was so brilliantly successful. The brisk, ingenious little piece sparkles in every line. The plot concerns the arrival at Old Goodwill's house of numerous relations : a doctor, a lawyer, a dancing-master, a singing-master, who all make proposals to marry the heiress. Miss Lucy, however, reveals at last that she has married the footman. Mrs. Clive had a charming voice and Fielding's talent as a song writer was never shown better than in this play for her.

> GOODWILL. Should you like to have a husband, Lucy ?
> LUCY. And am I to have a coach ?
> GOODWILL. No, no ! What has that to do with a husband ? . . .

LUCY. Then let me have the coach without this husband . . .
    Do you, papa, but find a coach,
    And leave the other to me, sir ;
    For that will make the lover approach
    And I warrant we shan't disagree, sir.
        No spark will talk
        To girls that walk,
        I've heard it and I confide in't ;
        Do you then fix
        My coach and six,
    I warrant I get one to ride in't, to ride in't.
    I warrant I get one to ride in't.

In 1734, Fielding at twenty-seven must have been in the very prime of youth, animated good looks and the gaiety that goes with high spirits and perfect health. In spite of distractions he had been, for three years at least, in love with the woman who was the passion of his life. Like all his inspiration, she came from the west country. She was Charlotte Cradock, the youngest of three pretty sisters who had a small fortune of their own and kept house together in Salisbury. Charlotte Cradock married him in 1734, and for ten years she experienced a degree of happiness and of suffering such as few women can have known in the same stretch of life.

The marriage of Henry and Charlotte Fielding was singularly happy, and one does not doubt it even when reading the tale of her exhaustion under illness, poverty, unusually painful confinements, loss of children, and the perpetual struggle to keep together a home for a man she adored, who combined extravagance, generosity and a total lack of any financial sense. The marriage was one of those of which it is said that they are made in Heaven, but ten years of it killed her.

Lady Bute, the daughter of Lady Mary Wortley Montagu,

speaking of her mother's recollections, said : " He loved her passionately and she returned his affection, yet had no happy life. For they were seldom in a state of quiet and safety. All the world knows what was his imprudence ; if he possessed a score of pounds, nothing could keep him from lavishing it idly, or make him think of the morrow."

Fielding has drawn his wife's portrait twice: once, five years after her death, as Sophia in *Tom Jones*, and again, seven years after, with undiminished brightness, as Amelia. When he has described Sophia, her white skin and vermilion blush, her gracefully curling black hair, her black eyes, that had " a lustre in them which all her softness could not extinguish," he says : " She was most like the picture of Lady Ranelagh, and, I have heard, still more to the famous Duchess of Mazarine ; but most of all, she resemble done whose image can never depart from my breast" (*Tom Jones*, Bk. IV, Chap. I), and in the preface to the thirteenth book, when he invokes his future fame, he says : " Foretell me that some tender maid, whose grandmother is yet unborn, hereafter when under the fictitious name of Sophia she reads the real worth that once existed in my Charlotte, shall from her sympathetic breast send forth the heaving sigh."

Among the lines addressed to Miss Cradock (published by Fielding in his *Miscellanies*) is this verse :

> Can there on earth, my Celia, be
> A price I would not pay for thee ?
> Yes, one dear precious tear of thine
> Should not be shed to make thee mine.

What a world of experience lies between this and such a passage as the following in *Tom Jones* : " To see a woman you love in distress and to be unable to relieve her, and at the same time to reflect that you have brought her into this situation is perhaps a curse of which no imagination can represent the horrors to those who have not felt it."

It has been sometimes objected that too dark a picture has been drawn of Fielding's worldly state in married life, and that Lady Mary viewed him too much in the light of a poor relation. Though the trials of poverty and misfortune were bitterly experienced, apart from the consolation of strong mutual love, the Fieldings had some periods of ordinary, mundane cheerfulness and well-being. One of these was in the years between 1734 and 1737 when they spent much of their time on a little country estate at East Stour in Dorset which Fielding had bought, partly with his wife's money. That his reckless hospitality and his style of living somewhat above the level of a simple country gentleman, brought this idyllic period to an end much sooner than it need have ended, appears probable. That it was deliciously happy while it lasted can be imagined from the echoes of it in " Mr. Wilson's Story " in *Joseph Andrews*.

Fielding was now working in the theatre as a family man who must make money. In 1736 he entered into management of the New Theatre in the Haymarket, which stood just beside the site of the present Haymarket Theatre. He had a play of his own for the opening season ; this was the formless but highly effective *Pasquin*. This piece has, as framework, the rehearsal of two plays, Mr. Trapwit's comedy, *The Election*, and Mr. Fustian's tragedy, *The Life and Death of Common Sense*. The first, enlarging on the theme already used in *Don Quixote*, shows the candidates in the town interest, Lord Place and Colonel Promise, *vis-à-vis* the country candidates, Sir Harry Foxchase and Squire Tankard. The election is conducted by the Mayor, and the Mayor's mind is made up for him by his wife and daughter.

As the latter have been captivated by Lord Place, Mrs. Mayor brings the town candidates in by the simple expedient of obliging the Mayor to reverse the actual result of the count, and to announce that the majority of votes were cast in their favour. The gravamen of the satire is of course in the electioneering scenes, as where Sir Harry Foxchase says :

> "And then we may provide for our friends ; I love my country, but I don't know why I may not get something by it as well as another, at least to reimburse me—And I do assure you, though I have not bribed a single vote, my election will stand me in a good five thousand pounds."

But there is also excellent comedy in the minor scenes, as between the two young ladies who are politically conscious:

> "Pray let me ask you seriously, are you thoroughly satisfied with this peace ? "
> "Yes, Madam, and I think you ought to be so, too."
> "I should like it well enough if I were sure the Queen of Spain were to be trusted."
> "Pray, Miss, none of your insinuations against the Queen of Spain ! "
> "Don't be in a passion, Madam—"
> "Yes, Madam, but I will be in a passion, when the interest of my country is at stake ! "

In the second piece, religion, in the person of the priest Firebrand, together with Law and Physic deserts from the Queen Common Sense and joins the invading army of Queen Ignorance. Beside the major satire, Fielding also holds up to ridicule, as he constantly does elsewhere, the public taste for pantomime, jugglers and rope-dancers, which were proving a serious rival to the legitimate stage. The author Fustian likewise gives a poignant account of the difficulties a playwright experiences in placing his play with a manager rehearsing it with captious actors, only to

have it damned on the first night, " where one man hisses
out of resentment to the author, a second out of dislike to
the house, a third out of dislike to the piece, a fifth [*sic*] for
the joke's sake and a sixth to keep all the rest in company."

This play was extremely popular, and had the then extraordinary run of forty consecutive nights. Fielding was
flushed with success and made plans to " enlarge and beautify "
his theatre. Assured prosperity seemed before him at last.
Then, in May 1736, he brought out another farce, *The
Historical Register*.

Walpole's government in spite of its long term of office
was harshly criticised, and in particular for the rank corruption of the methods Walpole employed. Indicating the
House of Commons, he had made his famous comment :
" All these men have their price." The Government had
taken a thorough pasting in *The Beggar's Opera* which con-
tinued its revivals since the original run in 1728. Fielding
had made his attacks on electioneering abuses in two plays,
of which *Pasquin* had been really dangerous by reason of
its popular success. *The Historical Register for the year* 1736
was less effective as a farce, but its satire was even fiercer.
It was composed of three episodes, again loosely related
in the framework of a rehearsal, Fielding's favourite device,
to which Sheridan was clearly indebted in *The Critic*,
though his debt to Buckingham's *Rehearsal* is the only one
usually recognised. The episode is a scene of five politicians
voting a tax ; the second, a brilliant little sketch of an auction,
in which the famous auctioneer of the day, Mr. Cocke,
is taken off as Mr. Auctioneer Hen, and puts up commodities
of Political Honesty, Patriotism, Modesty and Courage
for which he can scarcely raise a bid, then Lot 18, a very
considerable quantity of Interest at Court, for which a hundred

pounds is bid all over the room. There is an interlude in which the Cibbers, those well-tried comic favourites, make their appearance, Theophilus Cibber as Pistol, who has run mad and thinks himself a great man, and Colley Cibber as Mr. Ground Ivy preparing to rewrite *King John*. So far, there was nothing at which anyone could take offence. But the third episode cooked Fielding's goose. This was a scene depicting four patriots voting for peace or war : the noisy patriot, the cautious patriot, the self-interested patriot and the dormouse patriot, who, suddenly waking, says : " Here's to peace or war, I do not care which."

Mr. Quidam, who has been standing in the wings laughing, now enters upon the scene. This figure was immediately recognised as intended for Walpole. He throws a purse of gold on the table, and the patriots, cramming gold pieces into their pockets, assure him that they are all " convinced." Quidam then draws out his fiddle and dances off, with the patriots all dancing after him. It is explained that as each one of them has a hole in his pocket, Quidam will be able to pick up the gold pieces, and so be not a halfpenny the worse for his generosity.

The Ministry, during the past two years, had been considering some means of restraining theatrical satire. *The Historical Register* provided a decisive argument in favour of such a scheme. As additional support to the motion, Walpole himself showed round a play of indescribable indecency and scurrility called *The Golden Rump*, which, he said, he had bought up to prevent its being produced. There was some suspicion that he had caused it to be written. The proposed Licensing Act was not passed without great opposition ; many saw in it a sinister encroachment on freedom of speech, and Lord Chesterfield made an eloquent speech in defence of playwrights. It was, however, of no avail. The Bill was passed in July 1737. It limited the number of theatres and laid down that all dramatic writers must obtain a licence of the Lord Chamberlain. It was clear that Fielding's career as the manager of the New Theatre was over.

He had now a wife and at least one daughter to support. His infant son James had been buried in 1736. He was obliged to decide on some means of getting a solid livelihood. His legal family connections and his interrupted studies at Leyden, and no less, perhaps, his remarkable aptitude for the work, decided him to adopt the profession of a barrister. In 1737 he sold the little estate at East Stour where he and his wife had been so happy, the farms, orchards, meadowlands and copses, so that he might have something for his family to live on while he was reading for the Bar, and entered himself as a barrister at the Middle Temple.

In 1739, Colley Cibber brought out his *Apology*, in the eighth chapter of which his resentment against Fielding is displayed in a kind of muffled, high-minded manner. He refers to Fielding as " a broken wit," whose name he won't sink himself so far as to mention, though he hits off one happy sentence, that the wit, " to make his poetical fame immortal, like another Eratostratus, set fire to his stage by writing up to an Act of Parliament to demolish it."

Cibber had put his head into the lion's mouth. Fielding was by nature, and particularly when judged by the standards of the time, the least rancorous of men, but this quarrel he never allowed to drop. He was writing for a thrice-weekly paper, *The Champion*, at the time, and in one of the issues he arraigns *Col. Apol*, that, not having the Fear of Grammar before his eyes, he has been guilty of an outrage on his mother tongue. In each of his three novels and even in his final work, *The Journal of a Voyage to Lisbon*, he throws out humorous references to Cibber's *Apology*, ignoring, it is true, the admirable things it contains, but exposing its pretentiousness, its disingenuousness and its faulty grammar : attacks the more damaging because they read less like abuse than a hearty roar of laughter.

The Champion, an anti-Jacobite journal, was written largely by Fielding ; the papers were said to be contributed by different members of the Vinegar family, Dr. John Vinegar writing on medical matters, Mr. Noll Vinegar (who had once spent eighteen months considering one line of Horace) on questions of literary taste, Mrs. Joan Vinegar on housewifery and domestic matters. The character with which the public chiefly associated Fielding was Captain Hercules Vinegar, an observer on the times in general, whose club had the magic property of falling, of itself, on any knave in company. Fielding is several times gibed at by his opponents as " this *Herculean* satirist." Had they been his admirers, they could scarcely have chosen a better name for him.

Fielding said in *Amelia* (Chap. I) " To retrieve the ill consequences of a foolish conduct and by struggling manfully with distress to subdue it, is one of the noblest effects of wisdom and virtue." This retrieving, Fielding practised himself in the next three years. Mr. C. B. Jones has pointed out that whereas six years was the normal period of reading for the Bar, Fielding accomplished the study in exactly half the time, although he was now past thirty, when most men find application more difficult than in their undergraduate years. Murphy says of him at this time : " His application was remarkably intense, and though it happened that the early taste of pleasure he had taken would occasionally return upon him and conspire with his spirits and vivacity to carry him into the wild enjoyments of the town, yet it was particular in him that amidst all his dissipation nothing could suppress the thirst he had for knowledge . . . he has been frequently known by his intimates to return late at night from a tavern to his chambers, and there read and make extracts from the most abstruse authors for several hours before he went to bed ; so powerful were the vigour of his constitution and the activity of his mind."

The last number of *The Champion* under his editorship was published in 1740, the day before that on which Fielding was called to the Bar. He now " travelled the Western Circuit." His life, apart from his excursion to Leyden, had always been passed between London and the south-western counties. What he knew of the inns, landlords, landladies, chambermaids, coachmen, postillions and ostlers, of the Great West Road, was presently to be shown to all time. With all his powers, his industry, his anxious desire to provide for his family, he was to make a scanty living as a barrister, for he now became subject to agonising and prostrating attacks of gout. From thirty-three onwards his health was broken. It is not possible to say now what exactly was the matter with him and how far alcohol had brought it on ; we only know that the pace of his life was so hard, that he entered manhood with the physique and constitution of a giant, and had killed himself before he was forty-eight.

This phase of his existence brought him much misery ; his passionate love for his wife was the source of his most exquisite happiness but also, in poverty, of his keenest wretchedness. Not only was he frequently ill himself during these years and unable therefore to provide for her as he wished, but she herself, in spite of natural health and good spirits was sometimes very ill, and at least two of her children had died. Fielding speaks of her (*Miscellanies*) in these words : " I remember the most excellent of women and tenderest of mothers, when after a painful and dangerous delivery she was told she had a daughter, answering : ' Good God ! have I produced a creature who is to undergo what I have suffered ? ' and some years after, on the death of this same child, then one of the loveliest creatures ever seen, comforting herself with reflecting that her child could never know what it was to feel such a loss as she then lamented."

Mrs. Fielding's friends might have considered her marriage an unfortunate one, but one does not believe that she thought it so herself. Fielding's wonderful description of married love (*Tom Jones,* Bk. VI, Chap. I) which says how, though desire vanishes, the tenderest love remains, shows that he had experienced an ideally happy marriage, a state which is impossible unless both parties are comprehended in it.

Debarred as he was from making much money as a counsel, he earned some by " occasional " writing when he could. Among the published productions of the years 1741–42 is *A Full Vindication of the Dowager Duchess of Marlborough,* which he perhaps engaged in the more readily because his father had been one of Marlborough's generals. He also wrote a party poem addressed to Dodington, " On True greatness," which is remembered for the one line in which he describes his own figure as " a great, tattered bard," walking the streets.

The extremes of poverty and of wealth were not only much greater in the eighteenth century than anything which we now know, but they were much closer together. As the State made next to no provision for the relief of distress, the moment fortune began to turn, the abyss yawned, and the degrees of wretchedness and stark horror in its depths, which can scarcely be imagined by ourselves, were accepted then by every man and woman as among the facts of existence, even if they never expected to experience them in their own person. This perpetual violent contrast of luxurious elegance and death by starvation, gave to moral judgments a bolder hue than they bear to-day. To-day, the enlightened judgment has thrown aside such simple considerations as right and wrong. Thieves, whores and murderers are not to blame for their actions ; these are ascribed to heredity or neurosis, anything that remains to be accounted for being put down to environment. With us, good men are to be suspected and bad men excused. Whereas we see the varieties of human nature through a uniform greyish tint, the eighteenth century tended to see them in black and white.

A characteristic exponent of this view was Hogarth. The friendship between him and Fielding was of early growth. In 1731 Hogarth had designed the frontispiece for the published version of *Tom Thumb*. In *Joseph Andrews* and *Tom Jones*, Fielding describes the appearance of certain characters by referring the reader to some plate of Hogarth, and in the introduction to the former he pays Hogarth that famous compliment, that his people appear not only to breathe, but to think. Hogarth, too, drew the only picture of Fielding which is accepted as a likeness, although it was drawn from memory after the latter's death. Hogarth's series of pictures, " The Harlot's Progress " (1732), " The Rake's Progress " (1733), " Marriage à la Mode " (1745), "The Idle and the Industrious Apprentice" (1747), show at once the narrowness and the force of his convictions, and it is a tribute to his powers, that, under their spell, we not only share his convictions, but we feel his compassion.[1]

Fielding's social satire was infinitely subtler, his nature and genius much more elevated, than Hogarth's, but the connection between them, and Fielding's admiration for Hogarth's powers, make Hogarth's pictures a fascinating study for the light they throw on Fielding's taste. Furthermore, they give a graphic representation of reckless extravagance, poverty and misfortune, in the very shape in which Fielding must have seen them. Hogarth's picture of " The Distressed Poet," who sits clasping his head as he tries to write in the embrasure of the attic window, while his wife mends his coat and the dunning landlady stands at the door presenting her bill on a slip of formidable length, comes painfully to mind when Murphy speaks of the pressure of Fielding's distresses.

But out of scenes of pain, disappointment and anxiety, came one of the most exuberant works ever written. In 1742, Fielding published *The Adventures of Joseph Andrews and his Friend, Mr. Abraham Adams.*

It is hard for posterity to estimate the innovating genius at his true rate. We look back at him, as it were, across a foreground of development of which he contributed the origins. It is only by a careful consideration of the writings of Bunyan, Defoe and Swift, the only great names in English fiction before Richardson's, Sterne's, Smollett's and his own, that one can appreciate with any justice the profuse originality of the work Fielding put into the novel. He says in the preface to *Joseph Andrews* that his work is no more to be considered as a burlesque than Hogarth's. It is, however,

[1] Except perhaps in the last-mentioned series. The Idle Apprentice is bestial and revolting, and the Industrious Apprentice a nauseating prig.

a comic romance which differs from the serious romance " by introducing persons of inferior rank and consequently of inferior manners . . . and perhaps there is one reason why a comic writer should of all others be the least excused for deviating from nature, since it may not be always so easy for a serious poet to meet with the great and the admirable but life everywhere furnishes an accurate observer with the ridiculous."

The ridiculous, which he claims as the province of the comic romance, has never, he says, been described. He now defines it as the results which proceed from affectation of various degrees and kinds. " Great vices are the proper objects of our detestation, smaller faults of our pity, but affectation appears to me the only true source of the Ridiculous."

In 1740, Samuel Richardson had brought out *Pamela, or Virtue Rewarded*, and it was still at the height of its extraordinary success. This autobiographical romance of the servant-girl who holds off the would-be seducer, her master, and finally brings him to the point of marriage, deserved its success as an enthralling tale, if not the adulation it received as a work, second only to the Bible, said some, in instigating virtue. Not that Richardson's views are entirely untenable. It is true for instance that " Mr. B's " marriage to Pamela, when at last brought off, was one of love as well as passion, and that the love would never have grown had the passion been gratified as soon as it was felt. What then is wrong with *Pamela* ?

Fielding did not need to ask. His robust and masculine nature rejected the mind that prolonged, through a wilderness of correspondence, the prelude to a sexual climax. He had strong views about the seduction of innocent women (see *Tom Jones*, Bk. XIV, Chap. VII), but had he had a seduction in view, he would not have been held at arm's length through two volumes by such a sententious little humbug as Pamela. Richardson's hero is called throughout " Mr. B." Fielding called him Mr. Booby. He further ridiculed the whole situation of the novel by devising a brother for Pamela—Joseph—who retreated from the advances of Mr. B's aunt, the widowed Lady Booby.

It has often been pointed out that this design was abandoned after the opening chapters, and that in the unexampled brightness and animation that flood the work the characters move in an element of their own, with no trace of a parody. But the opening chapters were more than enough for Richardson. It was his nature to take himself very seriously, and this trait had been encouraged by the adulation of a crew of female readers. He suffered not only the anger of the artist, but the recoil of the puny, unexperienced male from a man of Fielding's temperament, with all the touchiness of the under-bred. That so silly a man could write so great a novel as *Clarissa* is one of the enigmas in what Fielding himself calls " the vast authentic book of nature." That he had much to forgive must be allowed, but he was incapable of forgiving it even when Fielding had paid a generous (and deserved) tribute to his next novel, *Clarissa*. It raged like the hectic in his blood and he pursued the works of his great rival with criticisms so venomous, and above all, so pointless and absurd, that even some of " his ladies," as he called them, occasionally demurred.

Fielding says that he owed much to Cervantes and Marivaux, and *Pamela* herself had come into the field before him, but nothing that he had gained from anybody else equalled his own contribution to the art of novel writing.

3

The framework of *Joseph Andrews* is loose—it is the peregrinating story on Cervantes' model. Joseph, a handsome, vigorous, innocent young man, promoted for his good looks to be Lady Booby's favourite footman, attends the family to town. At the death of Sir Thomas Booby, the widow makes advances to Joseph and turns him out of doors in vindictive jealousy when he does not respond. Joseph sets out on foot from London to return to the Booby family seat in the west country, where his sister the famous Pamela lives in the village, and his friend Parson Adams is the curate. At an inn on the route he falls in with Adams himself who is coming to town to get his sermons printed. Adams, discovering that he has left his manuscripts behind him after all, turns back with Joseph, and they continue their homeward journey together. One evening at twilight they come to the rescue, from some roughs, of a country girl who turns out to be Fanny, the fellow-servant whom Joseph loves, and who was coming to London to look for him as news had reached her that he was ill. The three friends meet with many adventures, of which the most material to the story is their encounter with Mr. Wilson, the quiet country gentleman who gives them hospitality for the night and tells them the story of his life. This story ultimately proves that Joseph is his son, stolen by gipsies and changed by them for Mrs. Andrews's infant girl, as the boy was by then pining and the girl was thriving. The gipsies afterwards sold this healthy child for three guineas to Sir Thomas, which was the origin of Fanny's being brought up in the Booby's household. The marriage of the young lovers and the bestowing of a living on Parson Adams, concludes the tale : but the story has as much relation to the book as a whole as the bones have to the flesh and blood, the breath and spirit, of man.

Like all great novelists, Fielding gives a double pleasure :—the sense of actuality, which Aristotle says is the pleasure of recognition, of saying : " That is he ! " and, added to this, the benefit of the artist's vision which guides our own. This special contribution of the artist is seen most clearly when he presents characters whose beauty we can understand when he points it out, but which we ourselves, who see the same thing but not with the same eye, might overlook.

The character of Parson Adams is the supreme achievement of *Joseph Andrews*, nor is there anyone to equal him in the greater novel that came after. Though in no sense modelled on Don Quixote, there is something Quixotic about him. He is said to have been inspired by the gauche, scholarly, absent-minded clergyman, Mr. Young of Gillingham in Dorset. Mr. Young had been a chaplain in Marlborough's army and during a campaign he wandered absently into the enemy's lines, his Æschylus in his hand. The French officers understood him at a glance, and instead of being put under arrest he was politely redirected to his company.

Parson Adams illustrates that combination of high intellect and extreme poverty which Johnson knew, and Robert Greene and Villon. He maintained a wife and six children on twenty-three pounds a year, and the meal in his cottage, at which he hands Fanny the bone of bacon he has been gnawing himself, is an illustration—like the description of his appearance—of the unsparing realism with which he is presented. The landlady, in denying that Parson Adams was in the inn, " had not erred designedly . . . she had unhappily mistaken Adams for a person travelling to a neighbouring fair with the thimble and button or some such other operation, for he marched in a swinging, great, but short white coat with black buttons, a short wig and a hat which so far from having a black band had nothing black about it."

Adams's lack of practical sense is nowhere better shown than in one of his earliest adventures. " He came to a large water which, filling the whole road, he saw no method of passing unless by wading through, which he accordingly did—up to the middle ; but was no sooner got to the other side than he perceived if he had looked over the hedge, he would have found a footpath capable of conducting him without wetting his shoes."

His unconscious dignity and moral stature are shown when he is made the victim of odious practical joking by the hangers-on of the squire, whose hounds had been encouraged to worry him. He says (*Joseph Andrews,* Bk. III, Chap. VII), " I apprehend my order is not the subject of scorn, nor that I can become so, unless by being a disgrace to it, which I hope poverty will never be called . . . my appearance might very well persuade you that your invitation was an act of charity, though in reality we were well provided for ; yes sir, if we had an hundred miles to travel, we had sufficient to bear our expenses in a noble manner (at which words he produced the half-guinea. . . .) I do not show you this out of ostentation of riches, but to convince you that I speak the truth."

His physical courage and his great strength, his wrist " of which Hercules need not have been ashamed," is equalled only by his tenderness and goodness of heart ; when Fanny turns faint at hearing Joseph's voice in the next room, Adams, who has been reading his manuscript volume of Æschylus, jumps up, and in his concern, throws it into the fire, " where Æschylus lay expiring . . . his dear friend which was the

work of his own hands and had been his inseparable companion for upwards of thirty years."

Of the male characters, second only to Parson Adams, is
Parson Trulliber. Fielding's eye for a gross and distorted
physique is like Hogarth's. It is said that the origin of this
individual was Mr. Oliver, the curate of Motcombe who
taught Fielding as a child before he went to Eton. The
bestial roughness and lowness of this parson who drove a
brisk trade as a hog-dealer, is one of the most startling pieces
of comedy in the book.

" The rotundity of his belly was considerably increased
by the shortness of his stature, his shadow ascending very
near as far in height when he lay on his back, as when he
stood on his legs. His voice was loud and hoarse, his accent
extremely broad. To complete the whole, he had a state-
liness in his gait when he walked not unlike that of a goose,
only he stalked slower."

Adams in his trustfulness no sooner hears that there is
a clergyman in the neighbourhood than he makes certain
of being lent the money to pay the innkeeper's bill. When
he presents himself at Trulliber's house the latter immediately
takes him for a hog-dealer, and forces Adams into the sty
to " handle " the hogs before he can get out a word, but,
" laying hold on one of their tails, the unruly beast gave
such a sudden spring that he threw poor Adams all along
in the dirt. Trulliber, instead of assisting him to get up,
burst into a laughter, and entering the sty, said to Adams
with some contempt, ' Why, dost not know how to handle
a hog ? ' " The picture is completed by the parson's wife,
who stands behind her husband's chair like a servant and when
Trulliber cries angrily to Adams : " Dost preach to me ? "
exclaims : " Ifacks, a good story, to preach to my master ! "

This view of a clerical family gives a disconcerting reminder of how odd it was possible to be in an age when rural districts were cut off from communication with the larger world.

Joseph Andrews has no charming female character of the eminent kind. The heroine—Fanny—is a picture of innocent sensuousness, modesty and sweet temper, but she is quite overshadowed by Parson Adams and by Joseph. The female masterpieces of the book are Lady Booby, the base, self-deceiving female rake, Mrs. Slipslop her waiting gentle-woman and the landlady Mrs. Tow-wouse.

Lady Booby, vacillating between lust and prudence, with her violent jealousy of poor Fanny, and the self-revelation of her conversation with Lawyer Scout, who tells her that the girl is as plain and dirty a creature as he ever saw, is a character which shows for the first time Fielding's unusual insight into the weakness of female nature. Mrs. Slipslop is on a much bolder scale ; she belongs to the circle of Mrs. Malaprop and Mrs. Gamp, both of whom perhaps owe something to her. Her appearance is alarmingly repulsive, " being very short and rather too corpulent in body, and somewhat red with the addition of pimples in the face. Her nose was likewise rather too long and her eyes too little, nor did she resemble a cow so much in her breath as in two brown globes which she carried before her." She united two characteristics which Fielding particularly disliked in women : a desire to appear learned, and a desire to force herself on a man who did not want her. In Mrs. Slipslop, both these tendencies become grotesque. Parson Adams " who durst not offend her by calling her words in question, was frequently at some loss to guess her meaning and would have been much less puzzled by an Arabian manuscript."

Her advances to Joseph are gruesomely comic : " ' If we like
a man, the lightest hint sophisticates whereas a boy proposes
upon us to break through all the regulations of modesty,
before we can make any oppression upon him.' Joseph,
who did not understand a word she said, answered : ' Yes,
Madam.' ' Yes, Madam ! ' replied Mrs. Slipslop with
some warmth, ' Do you intend to result my passion ? . . .
Barbarous monster ! How have I deserved that my passion
should be resulted and treated with ironing ? ' "

Mrs. Slipslop, however, as Fielding would have claimed,
is not a burlesque. There is an awful reality in her waddling
appearances, her driving up in coaches, and in her conversa-
tions even when they are not on the topic of her ruling passion,
as for instance her dialogue at the coach-door with Miss
Grave-Airs. " Miss Grave-Airs said : ' Some folks might
sometimes give their tongues a liberty to some people that
were their betters, which did not become them. For her
part, she was not used to converse with servants.' Slipslop
returned : ' Some people kept no servants to converse
with. . . .' Miss Grave-Airs cried : ' she believed her mistress
would not encourage such sauciness to her betters.' ' My
betters ! ' says Slipslop, ' who is my betters, pray ? ' ' I am
your betters,' answered Miss Grave-Airs, ' and I'll acquaint
your mistress.' At which Mrs. Slipslop laughed aloud and
told her : ' Her lady was one of the great gentry and such
little paltry gentlewomen as some folks would not easily
come at her.' "

The reverse side of Fielding's fondness for the women
he liked, is his appalling pictures of the ones he abominated.
The landlady Mrs. Tow-wouse is an ugly, cruel, lascivious
shrew whose portrait is equalled in ferocity only by that of
Mrs. Partridge in *Tom Jones*. When Joseph is brought

naked and bleeding to the inn, the landlord sends the chamber-maid to their bedroom for one of his shirts.

" ' Touch one if you dare, you slut ! ' said Mrs. Tow-wouse, ' your master is a pretty sort of a man to take in naked vagabonds and clothe them with his own clothes. I shall have no such doings. If you offer to touch anything I'll throw the chamber-pot at your head. . . .' ' My dear,' said Mr. Tow-wouse, ' this is a poor wretch.' ' Yes,' says she, ' I know it is a poor wretch. But what the devil have we to do with poor wretches ? . . .' ' My dear,' cries Tow-wouse, ' this man hath been robbed of all he hath.' ' Well, then,' said she, ' where's his money to pay his reckoning ? ' " The episode of the Tow-wouses is rounded off when Betty the chambermaid, who has fallen in love with Joseph and been gently repulsed by him, falls a prey to the desires of Mr. Tow-wouse and is discovered by Mrs. Tow-wouse in a compromising situation. The guests hear an uproar, " Mr. Tow-wouse, Mrs. Tow-wouse and Betty all lifting up their voices together, but Mrs. Tow-wouse's voice, like a bass viol in a concert, was clearly and distinctly distinguished among the rest." The situation was cleared up, and Fielding says that any reader of any experience, whether married or not, will imagine that it concluded " with the discharge of Betty, the submission of Mr. Tow-wouse, with some things to be performed on his side by way of gratitude for his wife's goodness in being reconciled to him, and lastly, his quietly and contentedly bearing to be reminded of his transgressions, as a kind of penance, once or twice a day during the residue of his life." (*Joseph Andrews*, Bk. I, Chap. XVIII.)

Fielding is a great comic writer, and by a paradox it is the greatest comic writers of whom we most often, in retrospect, fail to think as predominantly comic; perhaps because tragedy and comedy on the highest levels are both, in their different languages, saying the same thing. When one thinks about what Fielding says rather than how he says it, the impression is deeply serious. For instance, in the brilliant chapter : " A dissertation concerning high people and low people," where he says apropos of Mrs. Slipslop's refusing to recognise Fanny : " So far from looking on each other as brethren in the Christian language, they seem scarce to regard each other as of the same species. This, the terms ' strange persons, people one does not know, the creatures, wretches, beasts, brutes,' and many other appellations amply demonstrate, which Mrs. Slipslop, having often heard her mistress use, thought she had also a right to use in her turn, and perhaps she was not mistaken. For," he says, " as the house boy gets up early to brush the footman's clothes, the footman then brushes the valet's, the valet the squire's, the squire attends the lord's levee, the lord the favourite's and the favourite the sovereign's, so there is not, in that whole ladder of dependence, any one step at a greater distance from the other than the first from the second ; so that to a philosopher the question might only seem, whether you would choose to be a great man at six in the morning or at two in the afternoon."

Fielding said that Homer had written a comic epic which would have given the world a model of the comic kind, as he had already given one of the tragic, had not the comic epic unfortunately been lost. The scene in Lady Booby's house at the end of *Joseph Andrews*, where Beau Didapper steals to Mrs. Slipslop's bed in mistake for Fanny's, and Parson Adams, hearing a scream, rushes in the dark to the bedside, where, misled by the feel of the beau's delicate

skin and of Mrs. Slipslop's beard, he starts punching the
latter unmercifully, is a scene on what one might venture
to call a Homeric scale.

Fielding is not poetic, but he has a strong sense of the
beautiful, of moral beauty, the personal beauty of men,
women and children and of the countryside. He gives very
little expression to the last, but it is touching, when one
remembers how well he knew the road from London to the
West, to come upon the passage in *Joseph Andrews* (Bk. III,
Chap. V) where Adams, Joseph and Fanny, came " to one of
the beautifullest spots of ground in the universe. It was a kind
of natural amphitheatre, formed by the winding of a small
rivulet, which was planted with thick woods." " The whole
place might have raised romantic ideas in older minds than
those of Joseph and Fanny, without the assistance of love."

His conception of beauty is that of the Earthly Paradise.
Though he is frank, and can be gross, he conveys the height
of sensuous bliss with a kind of innocence. Smollett did
so too ; the wedding nights that close *Roderick Random*
and *Joseph Andrews* have a strangely lovely quality, though
it is not a spiritual one. Such scenes are much nearer to
the passion of Beaumont and Fletcher, of Shakespeare, even,
than to anything which comes after them. The scene is
particularly charming where Joseph, having rescued Fanny
from an attempt at kidnapping, in which the handkerchief
has been torn from her neck, stands transfixed with admiration at the sight of her bosom. But, seeing that she is uneasy
under his gaze, he removes his eyes, " so great was his fear
of offending her, and so truly did his passion for her deserve
the noble name of love."

Where so much is given to the reader, it is scarcely possible
to say what is the most remarkable of Fielding's many

powers ; but one, at least, of these, and it is the more striking
because he is a writer who works on a crowded canvas, is
that all his characters inhabit the same plane of reality.
Dickens, his great heir, is in some respects greater than he, but
here Dickens falls far short of him. Mrs. Slipslop and Fanny,
Tom Jones and Partridge, Parson Adams and Parson Trulliber,
Amelia and Miss Matthews, are, whether good or bad, pleasant
or unpleasant, respectable or idiotic, members of the same
world. It could never be said of Fielding that his heroes and
heroines were unconvincing, that his good characters were
less successful than his bad, or that certain scenes were of
the type he could draw, and others of a kind he could not.
Wide as his scope is, the *universality* of his imagination is
extraordinary. His respect for personality which made him
in later years uniquely sympathetic and efficient as a magistrate,
was of the first importance to him as an artist. It allowed
him, although he lived in an era of rigid class distinctions, to
throw off their influence when he looked at human nature.

The publisher, Andrew Millar, gave Fielding £185, 11s.
for *Joseph Andrews*. This did not go far in the support of
an ailing wife, children and a husband who was almost
incapacitated from earning anything by his profession.
Lady Mary Wortley Montagu's account of an existence of
" wretched garrets " and " sponging houses " has been
considered as a lively exaggeration ; but unsafe as it is to
attempt to deduce biographical detail from imaginative
works, one cannot but observe that in his two last novels,
those which admittedly give a picture of his wife, Fielding
dwells again and again on the misery a man endures who
knows that marriage to himself has brought poverty and
wretchedness to the woman he loves. Mrs. Fielding however
had one domestic comfort, apart from her husband ; this was

her devoted maid Mary Daniel. Either the household must have been able to pay Mary Daniel's wages, or there must have been periods when she nursed, cooked and cared for them for nothing. Fielding was not one of those who, when God sends a cheerful hour, refrains. Lady Mary Wortley Montagu said that : " His happy constitution (even when he had, with great pains, half-demolished it) made him forget everything when he was before a venison pasty or over a flask of champagne." He liked also to chew tobacco, and in 1743 there is a vivid little scene of his doing it. This story, told of Fielding, and by Garrick, contrives by their united energy, to burst the cerements of Murphy's fine writing and is the one truly graphic detail in his essay. In this year, an old and unacted play of Fielding's, *The Wedding Day*, was put on for Garrick, who was very doubtful about one of the scenes and said he was afraid it was not good enough to pass. Fielding, impatient, anxious and ill, said, " Let the public find that out ! " On the night, Garrick's apprehensions were justified by the hisses of the audience, and much shaken he came off into the Green Room, where Fielding was sitting. " He had by this time drank pretty plentifully ; and cocking his eye at the actor, while streams of tobacco trickled down from the corners of his mouth, ' What's the matter, Garrick ? ' says he. ' What are they hissing now ? ' ' Why, the scene that I begged you to retrench ; I knew it would not do ; and they have so frightened me that I shall not be able to collect myself again the whole night.' ' Oh, d—mn ' 'em,' replies the author, ' they HAVE found it out, have they ? ' "

Fielding's share of the proceeds of *The Wedding Day* was less than fifty pounds. Two months later, however, in April 1743, he published three volumes of *Miscellanies*. This collection of juvenalia, fragments and one major work, was preceded by a subscription list, which is remarkably interesting, not so much for the Prince of Wales's name which stands first but for the long list of eminent legal names, which shows that, however little Fielding's health allowed him to practise, he had made his mark with some of the most distinguished men of his profession. The publication brought him £700.

The first volume is more interesting for Fielding's sake than for its own, containing as it does, verses that he wrote when he was courting Charlotte Craddock, and older still, a verse translation of part of the *Sixth Satire of Juvenal*. This, he says, was "all the revenge taken by an injured lover," and is thought to be the relic of his attempt to carry off the heiress of Lyme when he was nineteen. The second volume contains an interesting fragment called *A Journey from this World to the Next*, and the introductory paragraph says he was drawn to study the half-indecipherable manuscript in which he pretends to have found it, because : " I have a surprising curiosity to read everything which is almost illegible, partly perhaps from the sweet remembrance of the dear Scrawls, Skrawls or Skrales (for the word is variously spelt) which I have in my youth received from that lovely part of the creation for which I have the tenderest regard." Two or three episodes in the traveller's journey are particularly interesting. One is the visit to the Palace of Death, of which the description of the Gothic pile, vast beyond imagination " of black marble surrounded by yews " is a singularly early example of the " gothic " horror which twenty years or so later was a commonplace. Within, the traveller finds that among memorials raised by Death to other great commanders, there is none to the Duke of Marl-

borough, because : " His Majesty hath no great respect
for the Duke, for he never sent him a subject he could keep
from him," : a saying that reminds one of the anecdote
Mr. Hardcastle was never allowed to finish, which began
at the siege of Denain, with the Duke's saying to George
Brooks, " I'll pawn my dukedom but I'll take that garrison
without spilling one drop of blood."

In the Elysian fields, the traveller, in Fielding's own
person, comes upon the heroes of antiquity, greeting the
authors who had written of them. " I now saw Ulysses
and Achilles addressing themselves to Homer, and Æneas
and Julius Cæsar to Virgil. Adam went up to Milton . . .
several applied themselves to Shakespeare, among whom
Henry V made a very distinguishing appearance. While my
eyes were fixed on that monarch, a very small spirit came
up to me, shook me heartily by the hand and told me his
name was Thomas Thumb."

His daughter Charlotte had died in 1741. He says :
" I presently met a little daughter whom I had lost several
years before. Good gods ! What words can describe the
rapture, the melting, passionate tenderness with which
we kissed each other, continuing in our embrace, with the
most ecstatic joy a space which, if time had been measured
here as on earth, could not be less than half a year." How
different is this from the anonymous author of *Pearl* who
saw his child in heaven and was rebuked by her for his
impious abandonment to grief. Both are heart-broken
fathers, but one is a doctrinaire and one a man.

Apart from these lines, perhaps the most beautiful Fielding
ever wrote, the most important part of the *Miscellanies*
is Volume Three which is filled by *The Life and Death of
Jonathan Wild the Great*.

This extraordinary story is unique among Fielding's works, not for its irony, its ferocity or the grimness with which it shows the life and habits of the criminal class ; all these elements he shows elsewhere ; but *Jonathan Wild* is unequalled in his work or the work of any other English writer except Swift, for the unrelieved intensity with which these qualities are displayed. The book is short and its impact is like a blow with a butcher's cleaver.

It has been suggested that the work was written a considerable time before it was published, in other words, that it is an earlier production than *Joseph Andrews*. That it is a much less brilliant work than the latter it is needless to say ; the characters are in most cases viewed so much from the outside that they present the appearance of type-characters galvanised by overwhelming force, rather than human beings. Irony is the mainspring of *Jonathan Wild* but tremendous though the book is as an ironic *tour-de-force*, there is nothing in it so effective as Fielding's casual remark in *Joseph Andrews*, on the postillion who gave his greatcoat to the robbed and naked Joseph Andrews when everyone of the coachful of passengers had declined to help him : "A lad who hath since been transported for robbing a hen-roost."

Fielding borrows the name of a criminal who was hanged at Tyburn in 1725, a thief who was also a thief-taker. He follows his career from childhood to the gallows, introducing Wild's background of thieves, highwaymen, card-sharpers, whores and the corrupt and brutal officials of Newgate, from the gaolers to the chaplain. His innocent victims, the jeweller Heartfree, his wife and children and their apprentice Friendly, by their simple virtue and affection, only throw the rest of the characters into deeper gloom.

The tale itself with its Hogarthian figures is an excellent

piece of story-telling, with the exception of Mrs. Heart-
free's adventures, related by herself at the end of the book.
These, by taking the reader to Africa, slacken the tension
of interest which was created inside the walls of Newgate.
The interpolation of stories within stories appears to be the
only weak device which Fielding borrowed from his contemporaries. Mrs. Heartfree's story is on a par with " The
Unfortunate Jilt " in *Joseph Andrews* and " The Man of the
Hill " in *Tom Jones*. Apart from this excrescence *Jonathan
Wild* is woven rapidly and with a firm yet spontaneous development of narrative. But good as the story is, it gains its
peculiar force from the method Fielding has used. The
work is, in Austin Dobson's celebrated phrase, " a model
of sustained and sleepless irony." Fielding has chosen the
rascal who is a " great man " in the lowest walks of life as an
illustration of the scoundrel who is a " great man " in the
highest rank of place and power. The gangster is con-
tinuously compared with the statesman, and the methods
and success of each serve throughout the book to illustrate
those of the other. He says he does not consider Newgate
" as no other than human nature with the mask off," but that
" the splendid palaces of the great are often no other than
Newgate with the mask on." Wild, when his accomplice
Bagshot who has committed a robbery at Wild's instigation
demurs to his appropriating the whole of the booty, says :
" It is well said of us, the higher order of mortals, that we
are born only to devour the fruits of the earth, and it may as
well be said of the lower class that they are born only to
produce them for us. Is not the battle gained by the sweat
and danger of the common soldier ? Are not the honour
and fruits of the victory the general's who laid the campaign ?
Is not the house built by the labour of the carpenter and the

bricklayer ? Is it not built for the profit only of the architect and for the use of the inhabitant, who could not easily have placed one brick upon another ? . . . Why should the state of a prig (thief) differ from all others ? Or why should you, who are a labourer, expect a share of the profit ? "

The theme of " greatness " (" a great man in society is like a wolf in a sheepfold " says one of the prisoners in Newgate) is emphasised at every opportunity ; the system of the gangster is traced in every walk of life, and particularly in the highest. The victimisation and suffering of every decent person in the book (except the magistrate who appears as the *deus ex machina* at the end), the arrogance, cruelty and utter wickedness of the gangster chief (hideously familiar to all who have seen the rise of Hitler), give a picture of the rule of wrong operating throughout society which in its gloom is scarcely equalled outside the ravings of King Lear ; and yet the work is presented in the medium of comedy.

Parts of *Jonathan Wild*, even, are sheer entertainment. The hero becomes enamoured of Miss Laetitia Snap, who with her sister Theodosia are the daughters of Mr. Snap, who combines the occupation of sheriff's officer with those of thief-taker and fence. Wild's lust for this dirty, promiscuous and ill-natured slut, its rapid satiety and the dialogue of the couple in their bed one morning, are pieces of superb comic writing.

One of the rare passages in the book which are not ironic, shows Fielding's attitude to women at its best. The horrible Laetitia, hearing that her sister has had a child by Count La Ruse, urges their father to turn her out of doors, " being resolved never to set her foot over the same threshold with the trollop, whom she detested so much the more because (which was perhaps true) she was her own sister."

4

The wretched Theodosia was removed to Bridewell " where she suffered so much correction for her crime, that the good-natured reader of the male kind may be inclined to compassionate her, at least to imagine she was sufficiently punished for a fault which, with submission to the chaste Laetitia and all other strictly virtuous ladies, it should either be less criminal in a woman to commit, or more so in a man to solicit her to it."

Fielding seems to have begun to acquire his knowledge of the faulty workings of the law early in life. In *Rape upon Rape* the characters of Justice Squeezum and the gaoler attest this. By the time, whatever time it was that *Jonathan Wild* was written, this knowledge had become encyclopædic. In this novel he gives a conspectus of the whole system of criminal law, with particular emphasis on its administration inside the gaol. The prison officials of whom he gives a full-length picture are uniformly corrupt and bad. The climax of his description is the revolting callousness of the officer in command of the execution, who charges the condemned Heartfree five guineas to spend ten minutes with his fainting wife, and then twenty guineas to make it an hour—before disclosing that Heartfree's reprieve has arrived in the meantime. The explanation of this state of things, as pointed out by Mr. C. B. Jones, is that the post of gaoler had as a rule no salary attached to it, the gaoler being expected to extort money in fines and exactions and pillaging of every kind from the imprisoned victims ; " down to 1730 the office was bought and sold, £5000 being given for the Wardenship of the Fleet Prison." [1]

Heartfree is released and Wild arrested, through the turning King's evidence of Wild's accomplice, Fireblood ;

[1] C. B. Jones, *Fielding, Novelist and Magistrate*.

a state of things brought about through the aroused suspicions of one of the few capable magistrates who appear in Fielding's works. There is more than a hint of what admirable service Fielding was later to render to the community, in the account of Fireblood's original evidence on which Heartfree was committed.

" Mr. Fireblood was soon produced to bear testimony for his friend which he did with so much becoming zeal and went through his examination with much coherence (*though he was forced to collect his evidence from hints given him by Wild in the presence of the justice and the accusers*——)."

The study of Wild's character which is the mainspring of the story is conceived with considerable depth. Its most striking attribute is the consistency with which he follows the rule of self-interest and the strength of personality with which he is able to subdue all other interests to his own. Complete consistency in such respects would however be unnatural, and Fielding shows the monster enduring, brief though it is, and soon mastered, a kind of agony when he hears that Heartfree is to be hanged. Otherwise, Wild's consistency is unimpaired and he offers a fine example of " the ruling passion, strong in death." At the foot of the gallows, while the parson was reading a prayer, Wild "applied his hands to the parson's pocket, and emptied it of his bottle screw, which he carried out of the world in his hand."

The character of Peachum in *The Beggar's Opera* was said to have been founded upon the actual Jonathan Wild ; at the same time, it was considered to embody a satire upon Walpole. Fielding's Jonathan Wild also has often been said to reflect upon Walpole. That there is nothing in the picture of Wild to suggest Walpole's own character is self-evident, but the continuous holding up to execration of power and corruption, combined in the hands of one "great man" may have been sufficient to suggest to contemporaries the image of the supremely powerful minister who was notorious for the corruption of his administration. If this were so, it might lend some significance to the date at which *Jonathan Wild* was published, for Walpole went out of office the previous year.

Of Fielding's numerous brothers and sisters, two only seem to have had any intimate connection with him. One was his own sister Sarah, three years younger than himself, and the other his half-brother John, who was blind from birth, but who had inherited, if not the genius, the courage and initiative that distinguished his half-brother. In spite of his dire handicap, John Fielding played his part as an important citizen. He became a justice of peace, and it was said of him that he could tell over three thousand thieves by their voice.

Sarah Fielding must have been a very charming creature because her brother thought so in spite of his prejudice against learned women. She had been taught Latin and Greek and translated Xenophon's *Memoirs of Socrates*.

In 1744, she published a long short-story, *David Simple, containing an account of his travels through London and Westminster in search of a Friend*. This spritely and sensible, yet tedious moral tale has one recommendation—Fielding wrote the preface.

This introduction tells the reader much more about Fielding's affection for his sister, than of what he will find in the pages of *David Simple*. When Fielding says that certain touches in the work might have done honour to the pen of Shakespeare, one can but feel that this is simply not the case. Yet this judgment is scarcely wider of the mark than Richardson's, when he told Sarah Fielding that her knowledge of human nature exceeded Fielding's own ; confronted with these enigmas of contemporary criticism, it must be safe to say that few people can have thought so at the time and nobody thinks so now.

Despite his over-favourable estimate of the book, Fielding's preface is a most charming thing. He makes a point of denying that he had anything to do with the writing of the book, and it is strange that anyone who had read it should have supposed he had. He says : " If she had wanted any assistance of mine I should have been as ready to have given it to her." As it was, all he had contributed were " two or three hints which arose on the reading of it and some little direction as to the conduct of the second volume." He says : " There were some grammatical and other errors in style in the first impression, which my absence from town prevented my correcting, but these," he says, " were small errors which want of habit in writing chiefly occasioned." The attitude of a protective and kindly elder brother is not yet out of date, but all Fielding's sympathy with the oppression of the female sex will not reconcile feminists to him when he goes on to say : " and which no man of learning would think worth his censure in a romance, nor any gentleman in the writings of a young woman." The preface afforded him an opportunity, besides that of doing a service to " one . . . nearly and dearly allied to me, in the highest friendship and relation," of making a very important statement about himself. In disclaiming any part of the authorship of *David Simple*, he reminded the public of a promise he had solemnly made in print, " of never publishing even a pamphlet without setting my name to it." He was now so well-known a literary figure, that anonymous scurrilities of many kinds were ascribed to him by his enemies. The most flagrant instance of this was the fathering upon him of a set of verses called *The Causidicade* which slandered some of the most eminent legal men of the day. The retirement of Sir John Strange had left vacant the office of Solicitor-General, and this lampoon pretended to contain the setting forth of his own claims in a highly indecent manner by each of the possible candidates. As some of the distinguished lawyers so attacked were those who had subscribed to the publication of the *Miscellanies*, Fielding found this libel infuriating to the last degree. He says that those who called him the author of *The Causidicade* " accused me not only of being a bad writer and a bad man, but with downright idiotism in flying in the face of the greatest men in my profession."

In this year Charlotte Fielding died. Lady Mary says that " she declined, caught a fever and died in his arms." As to Ezekiel, God said : " I take away from thee the desire of thine eyes." For a time, Murphy says, Fielding's friends thought that he would lose his reason. The faithful Mary Daniel took care of the children and took care of him. His only consolation was in talking to her about his wife, and they wept together.

Two children appear to have survived the marriage, a boy and a girl. In 1745, the rebellion of Prince Charles Edward caused a precipitation of Whig and Jacobite feeling, and Fielding entered journalism once again, in the anti-Jacobite journal, *The True Patriot*. One of its papers gives a glimpse of himself, as he sat in his study, " meditating for the good and entertainment of the public, with my two little children (as is my usual course to suffer them) playing near me."

In 1746, he for a time joined households with his sister Sarah, in Beaufort Buildings, off the Strand. It was here that Warton spent two evenings with him. " The lady," says Warton, " retired early," but he and his friend then had such an enchanting spell of Fielding's conversation, bereaved and ill though he was, that they did not get to bed till between one and two in the morning. It was of this household too that the famous anecdote is told of a pressing demand from the tax collector, and of Fielding's going to borrow the money from Andrew Millar. On his return, his sister asked anxiously whether he had got it ? But Fielding on his way back had met an old friend whom he had not seen for many years and who was now in want. He told his sister : " Friendship had called for the money. The tax collector must call again."

Fielding's life contained many misfortunes but he had amazing good fortune in one respect. The women with whom he was intimately connected loved him dearly and made him happy. Of Charlotte Fielding, the first and fairest, the bright image irradiates his greatest work. His happy relations with his sister Sarah were witnessed to by himself. In the faithful Mary Daniel, who had taken care of his wife, his children and himself, he found another companion. The agonies of grief which she had shared with him and in which she had supported him, created their inevitable bond. It is often found that the most inconsolable of widowers will not be long in forming a new attachment, because he is unable to bear his loneliness. Fielding's was a case in point. In November 1747, three years after his wife's death, he married Mary Daniel, and their son was born three months later. The marriage was approved of by some of his best friends, and George Lyttelton gave the bride away, but it was sneered at in some quarters. Smollett, in his vitriolic animosity to Fielding, for which the most probable, if subconscious cause would seem to be envy at a genius much greater than his own, commented on the marriage in a paragraph in *Peregrine Pickle*, which he afterwards suppressed :

" When he is inclined to marry his own cook-wench his gracious patron may condescend to give this bride away ; and may finally settle him in his old age as a trading Westminster Justice."

The paragraph is interesting because of the latter prophecy, inspired no doubt by what was already in the air. In December 1748, Fielding was appointed Justice of Peace for Westminster.

On his second marriage, Fielding removed to a small house in Twickenham, in what was called Back Lane. That the marriage was happy we know on the best authority—his own. Beauty, and the inspiration of passionate love, had vanished from his life ; but kindness, practical good sense and absolute, submissive devotion to his comfort, were left him. Hogarth made a drawing of Mary Fielding which is unfortunately lost ; someone who saw it described it as " the excellent likeness of a plain woman." A plain woman, in its wider sense, is a good description of what she was. He could scarcely have been more fortunate.

Fielding was now forty. The racking pains of gout had broken his once buoyant vigour. Sickness and grief had made their mark even on his high spirits and splendid frame. Yet he was in his prime, and it was an immortal one. In 1749, Andrew Millar brought out *Tom Jones*.

The novel is a work whose end has always been the giving of pleasure ; hence the low estimation in which certain people have held and hold it still. The greatest novels are those of which it is the most difficult to convey any adequate impression ; they should not be read about, but read. Their essential quality, readability, can no more be described than scent or music.

Fielding's genius is the incommunicable charm ; half a page of *Tom Jones*, opened upon at random, will stimulate the reader's appetite more effectively than chapters of exposition ; but Fielding was not only a great artist : in *Tom Jones* he shows himself the greatest craftsman who ever attempted the English novel, and it is this secondary feature of his work of which a study can be made with some success.

Nothing is more significant in the development of the novel in our own time, than the fact that story-value has been relegated to the lower ranks of writers. A good story is now the mark of your best-selling popular novel, not of the novel which is a *succès d'estime*.

Fielding, a great novelist, was also a great master of plot. Murphy said his plays were ill-constructed, but though his theatrical experience may not have taught him to construct a good plot for the stage, it had undoubtedly taught him how to construct the plot of a novel. Loosely constructed as *Joseph Andrews* is, it is told with a strongly developed narrative skill. *Jonathan Wild* proceeds on a complicated but symmetrical track of its own ; neither book, however, prepares the reader for the amazing *tour-de-force* of plot-construction in *Tom Jones*. Coleridge said there were three perfect plots in the world : those of *Œdipus Tyrannus, The Alchemist* and *Tom Jones*. The windings and unwindings of the narrative are perpetually felt by the reader as a stimulus to the interest, but unless he has a mind of great grasp, he is unlikely to appreciate the ingenuity of the whole at a first reading. Nor is it necessary to the enjoyment of the novel that he should. The purpose of the watch's works is that we should be able to read the time on its face. Our being able to tell the time is something quite different from our having a profound knowledge of the wheels and springs.

The centre of the story is the house of Mr. Allworthy in Somerset, where Allworthy kept an open table, as his prototype, the wealthy, self-made Allen, kept it at Prior Park. The rich, kindly, somewhat slow-witted Allworthy, a widower, lives with his unmarried sister Bridget, who was, says Fielding, exactly like the lean, ill-humoured gentlewoman who is walking to church in the wintry weather of Hogarth's print called " Morning." Miss Allworthy comes upon the scene at once as an unhappy and disappointed woman. Though plain and unattractive : " her prudence was as much on the guard as if she had all the snares to apprehend which were ever laid for her whole sex." Fielding adds : " This guard of prudence like the trained bands, is always readiest to go on duty when there is least danger." The story opens with Mr. Allworthy's returning late from London one evening, and being about to get into his bed when he finds a baby boy lying in it. Allworthy is rapt " in contemplating the beauty of innocence, appearing in those lively colours in which infancy and sleep always display it." He sends for the housekeeper Mrs. Wilkins, who, another virtuous woman, exclaims : " Faugh, how it stinks ! It doth not smell like a Christian," and is for sending the child out of the house " as if it were some noxious animal," but Allworthy, besides being worked on by his natural goodness of heart, " had now got one of his fingers into the infant's hand, which by its gentle pressure, seemed to implore his assistance." The child is brought up in his house, Miss Allworthy kindly undertaking the care of it.

She herself is presently courted by one of the hangers-on of Allworthy's hospitality, the coarse and evil Captain Blifil. A child is born of this marriage, and shortly afterwards the odious Captain Blifil dies of apoplexy. Meanwhile the foundling's parentage has presumably been discovered. The father is assumed to be one Partridge, the local schoolmaster with a ferocious wife, who, Fielding says, was exactly like the servant pouring out tea in Plate IV of " The Harlot's Progress." The mother is said to be a plain and bookish girl called Jenny Jones who was Mrs. Partridge's maid and to whom the schoolmaster had been teaching Latin. Jenny Jones disappears, Partridge is driven from the neighbourhood, and Tom Jones and Master Blifil are brought up together in the great house. Their education is carried on by the learned, conscientious but brutal chaplain, Thwackum, (who looked exactly like th overseer in Bridewell in " The Harlot's Progress," Plate V), and the philosopher Square, another of the pensioners on Allworthy's bounty. The social circle is closed by the family of Squire Western, the great neighbouring landowner, his sister Miss Western, the eminent feminist and politician, and his daughter Sophia who is a year or two younger than the boys. A family of great importance, not in the social scale, but to the plot, is that of Allworthy's gamekeeper Black George Seagrim, his wife and daughters. The stage thus set, the second phase of the story opens, when Tom is nineteen, Blifil eighteen and Sophia seventeen.

Though the plot is a very elaborate structure, its basis nevertheless is the characters of the three young people, of which Tom's is the most important. Fielding, in dedicating the novel to Lyttelton, says : " I have endeavoured strongly to inculcate that virtue and innocence can scarce ever be injured but by indiscretion, and that it is this alone which often betrays them into the snares that deceit and villiany spread for them." It is the open, exuberant, unsuspicious nature of Tom, exploited by the utterly contrary nature of Blifil, that motivates the plot.

Blifil, the frigid hypocrite, the conscienceless, heartless cheat and liar, is drawn with an effect of force held in reserve. Seeing how very important a part he plays, he appears comparatively little. When he does appear, it is as if the reader viewed him at a little distance. Nevertheless, he is seen quite near enough. Fielding does not trouble to analyse Blifil's heredity, but he has given the story of it—the embittered, unsatisfied mother, the coarse and greedy father, his parents' mutual hatred—Blifil though atrocious is not only credible but accounted for. The episode of childhood, where he lets loose Sophia's bird out of spite, and pretends that he did it from kindness to the creature, while Tom curses him, and climbing along a branch after it, falls into the canal, is one of those illuminations of character by a single instance which Fielding constantly produces. Though he was not interested in morbid psychology, Blifil's courtship of Sophia shows what Fielding could do with it if he liked. Blifil knows that Sophia detests him, " nor was his desrie at all lessened by the aversion he discovered in her to himself. On the contrary, this served rather to heighten the pleasure he proposed to himself in rifling her charms, as it added triumph to lust ; nay, he had some further views, from obtaining the absolute possession of her person, which we detest too much even to mention, and revenge itself was not without its share in the gratifications which he promised himself." (Bk. VII, Chap. VI.)

The character of Tom is a most original one for a hero,

at a time when the heroic convention was in full force. Nowadays we are accustomed, more often than not, to the hero who is a criminal, or at best a neurotic cad, but Tom is cast in the antique heroic mould in that he has superb physique, great personal beauty, high courage and an open nature. He is both loving and beloved, but he is also violently sensual and for the greater part of the book he prefers to err first and be very sorry afterwards, rather than to avoid the fault by any effort of self-control. His courage as a boy in refusing to betray Seagrim after a poaching expedition, in spite of Thwackum's most brutal flogging, is heroic ; but it was he who, mad for sport, insisted on following the bird on to Squire Western's land, although he knew that ruin for Seagrim and his family would be the result if the latter were caught breaking the game laws.

The most touching part of his nature is his affection. As a small child, he had loved even Blifil. His love and gratitude to Allworthy are so intense, that when, through the adroit exploitation and the machinations of Blifil, Allworthy turns him out of the house, Tom's grief forms the most moving passage in the book. He flings himself on the grass in a paroxysm of weeping, and his grief is so utterly devoid of any selfish feeling, that, when at last he gets up, he leaves behind him on the grass the pocket-book with the bank-note for £500 which Allworthy has given him as a final bounty.

It is the working on the better side of his nature of his love for Sophia that redeems his character. His early friendship for Sophia is innocent of passion because he has been seduced by Molly Seagrim. He is at first conscious only of admiration, affection and respect. By the time his passion is aroused, he realises that though Sophia loves him, his love can bring her only ruin and disaster. One of Fielding's boldest and most brilliant effects in this study of human nature is the celebrated passage in which Tom is meditating in the most high-wrought manner on Sophia's charms and telling himself that it is impossible any other woman should have an attraction for him, when Molly Seagrim, who has been hay-making, " without a gown, in a shift that was somewhat of the coarsest and none of the cleanest, bedewed likewise with some odoriferous effluvia, the product of the day's labour," approaches with a pitchfork in her hand, and within a few moments Tom has retired with her into the bushes. It is Fielding's triumph that he traces the evolution of such a young man into the tender and constant husband of Sophia, even though, in Tom's later stage, a distinguished critic has called him " the fortunate—the too fortunate—Mr. Jones."

Tom's casting off by Allworthy starts him on the road to Bristol, for he means to go to sea, and is only deflected in his purpose by falling in with a troop of redcoats who are mustering to oppose the Pretender in the 'Forty-Five. Blifil's suit to Sophia, violently urged by her father, causes Sophia to run away with her maid Honour. She intends to make her way to London, to the protection of her kinswoman Lady Bellaston. Thus the hero and the heroine are both upon the road—in Fielding's favourite milieu.

The character of Allworthy, founded partly on Lyttelton's and partly on that of Ralph Allen, though in quieter tones than the rest of the book, is very successful. Allworthy has an excellent heart and temper, and one of the most touching moments of the book is when Tom is in the depths of misfortune and supposed disgrace, and Allworthy, recalling the exquisite description of Tom as a baby asleep in his bed, exclaims in a passion of grief : " I still remember the innocent, the helpless situation in which I found him. I feel the tender pressure of his little hands at this moment. He was my darling, indeed he was." Fielding puts into Allworthy's mouth, with perfect verisimilitude, an argument against the wickedness of forced marriage, which was far beyond the general attitude of the age. Allworthy says that though he would be most happy to see Sophia married to Blifil, he will not be party to any coercion of her, for " to force a woman into a marriage contrary to her consent or approbation is an act of such injustice and oppression that I wish the laws of our country could restrain it. . . . To discharge the matrimonial duties in an adequate manner is no easy task. . . . Shall we tear her very heart from her, while we enjoin her duties to which a whole heart is scarce equal ? " Yet with all these good qualities, we suspect in Allworthy just that degree of stupidity which makes it credible that he could have Blifil and Tom under his roof for so long, and yet know so little of the character of either.

His neighbour, on the contrary, is drawn in violent colours. The overpowering character of Squire Western, his boisterousness, his grossness, his determination that his daughter shall marry whom he pleases even if she hangs herself the next morning, are astoundingly combined with a kind of innocence, and a genuine love for Sophia, which is not only believed in by Sophia herself, but is even recognised by the reader. Squire Western justifies, if ever man did, the Yorkshire saying : " There's nowt so queer as folk." His sister, Miss Western, who stands with her back to the fire taking snuff and lards her conversation with the doings of the army of Louis XIV, is almost as ridiculous in her own way as the Squire in his, and yet Sophia, a girl of quiet but sound good sense, respects and loves them both ; a wonderful illustra-

tion of the strength of family affection. At the height of
her father's anger with her, when he has locked her into her
room, she is alarmed by the sounds of an assault made on
him downstairs, and screams out in terror for him. When
he unlocks the door, she grasps his hand and can only say :
" O my dear sir, I am frightened to death ! I hope to heaven
no harm hath happened to you."

The most brilliant part of the book is perhaps that concerned with Tom's adventures on the road from Gloucester to
London. One after another the episodes throw out, bursting
with animation and yet pointed by the artist's selective
skill, seemingly inconsequent, but each one linked either
to something that has gone before or to what is yet to come.
When Tom's head has been broken by an ensign's throwing
a bottle at him, because he resented a disrespectful comment
on Sophia, the travelling barber-surgeon who dresses it
turns out to be none other than Partridge, who, supposing
Tom to be Allworthy's bastard heir under a temporary
cloud, decides to throw in his fortunes with him. The
character of Partridge, base, contemptible and maddeningly
irritating as it is, is perhaps the *chef-d'œuvre* of the entire book.
Though he is utterly ignoble, he challenges comparison with
Parson Adams himself, because of the scale on which he is
conceived. The *intense* quality of his stupidity, his indiscretion, his untrustworthiness, his dog-like cheerfulness and
gregariousness, makes one of those pictures of humanity
that only genius can produce. A typical instance of his
behaviour occurs in the inn at Upton, when Tom and Sophia,
unbeknown to the former, are actually under the same roof,
and Sophia runs away because her maid tells her that Partridge
has said in the tap-room that Sophia has made such a set at
Tom, he is going to the wars to be rid of her. When he

learns what Partridge has done, Tom threatens to kill him, and the reader almost wishes that he would. Yet it is Partridge who is the medium of that magnificent compliment to Garrick's acting, when Tom takes him to see *Hamlet*, and Partridge is terrified of the ghost, because he sees the little man upon the stage is so much frightened of it. And he pooh-pooh's Tom's suggestion that the greatest actor is taking the part of Hamlet, because, he says, any man would have behaved just as he did. " The King for my money," he says, " he speaks his words twice as loud again as any of the others. Anyone may see *he* is an actor."

The whole adventure of the inn at Upton is the keystone of the arch. Tom, at the time of Sophia's arrival, is in bed with Mrs. Waters whom he had rescued on the way from the dastardly Ensign Northerton (the same who had broken Tom's head with a bottle), who had robbed and was hanging her. The gentleman, in pursuit of a runaway wife, who bursts into the bedroom, mistakenly thinking that Mrs. Waters is she, is in fact the odious husband of Sophia's cousin, Harriet Fitzpatrick. This wandering and benighted young lady overtakes Sophia in a dark and windy lane, and, on their becoming known to each other in the darkness, they join forces and make their way towards London together. Tom, following down the identical lane some hours later, meets a cripple at the cross-roads who offers him for sale the little gilt pocket-book dropped by Sophia when she pulled out her handkerchief to tie on Mrs. Fitzpatrick's hat. The return of the pocket-book, which contains a bank-note, is Tom's excuse for tracing Sophia and presenting himself when he gets to London.

The London phase of the story, in which the adventures of all the characters are concluded, is remarkable for Tom's

5

part in the fortunes of the family of Mrs. Miller, with whom
he takes up lodgings, and for his affair with Lady Bellaston,
who meets him while he is searching out Sophia.   Mrs.
Miller, a widow with two daughters, is a protégée of Allworthy's, and has been set up in a lodging-house by him,
for which she makes the token payment of having rooms for
him whenever he comes to town.   The widow's anxious
struggle to support her daughters and establish them is at
once communicated to the reader, and it is with a sense of
dismay that one discovers that the older daughter Nancy,
a small, pretty, delicate girl of sixteen, has been got with
child by the lodger, young Mr. Nightingale, and that
Nightingale refuses to marry her, partly for fear of his father's
displeasure, and partly because, though he is really fond of
the girl, he is afraid he will be thought a fool if he marries
a whore, even though she is his own.   Tom's arguments
and expostulations with young Nightingale are an admirable
exposition of the philosophy of the loose-liver who is also
a decent man.   They not only convince Nightingale that
he must do the proper thing, but they give a very welcome
view of Tom's own nature. He draws the distinction between
a woman of the world who can take care of herself, and an
innocent, trusting girl ; between a robust-tempered female
to whom one man is no more than another, and a tender-
hearted child like Nancy Miller whose entire life will be
ruined by an affair with a selfish profligate. Young Nightingale, in his heart, wants to be convinced, and Tom's success
in bringing about the marriage and even a reconciliation
with Nightingale's family, gives him such a heroic partisan
in Mrs. Miller, that the good woman does him much service
with Allworthy when the latter comes to town with Blifil.

The episode which arouses so much criticism is Tom's

affair with Lady Bellaston. The latter is one of Fielding's horrifying pictures of women : an elderly lady of fashion of lascivious temperament, painted and with bad breath. Tom is reduced to his last penny and when Lady Bellaston sends him money and a masquerade ticket, he allows himself to be drawn into a liaison with her though his personal feelings are those of unmitigated discomfort and dismay. His natural gallantry which makes it second nature to him to be agreeable to women, his abounding vitality and his unselfconscious attitude to the sexual function, make him an easy prey to a wealthy experienced mondaine who is determined to buy a lover. The one extenuation is, that, as a young man fresh from the country and new to Grosvenor Square, he thought Lady Bellaston really loved him, and for the time being felt that he owed her consideration on this account. When young Nightingale relates some experiences of a friend of his with Lady Bellaston, Tom is undeceived as to the real nature of her feelings. The matter of a hero's allowing such a woman as Lady Bellaston to give him money in consideration of going to bed with her, which is what it amounts to, produces such indignation on the one hand, and such a desire to extenuate him on the other, that criticism is apt to become a little irrelevant. The point is surely, not whether Tom ought or ought not to have taken the money. Everyone will agree that he should have hired himself out as a porter in Covent Garden rather than have accepted Lady Bellaston's guineas. But, if we cease to think about whether Tom ought to have done it, and ask, merely, whether he would have done it, the answer seems plain. Nor does it make him seem altogether odious. In the horrid maze of this affair, the reader pities him sincerely. In the preface to Book X, Fielding warns us not to condemn a character as a bad one because it is not a perfectly good one. It is true that what affects the moral taste is not the seriousness, but the type, of fault. A hero would suffer less in his reputation if he committed a murder, than he does in becoming Lady Bellaston's kept man. But Fielding is drawing a human being and not a pattern, and Tom's faults have to be accepted and taken for granted as we recognise our friend's faults and our own. To try to write off the episode, is to pay a tribute to the lovable nature Fielding has created, but it is also to belittle the breadth of his portrait.

In the denouement, the action is closely packed and rapidly moving ; Tom is imprisoned for supposed manslaughter in an affray engineered between Lady Bellaston and Lord Fellamar, both equally concerned in keeping Tom away from Sophia. The reappearance of Mrs. Waters discloses that she is none other than Jenny Jones, and thus for a short time Tom has to bear the crowning catastrophe of thinking he has committed incest. This nightmare is dispelled by Mrs. Waters's own story. She reveals that the foundling was not her child, but Bridget Allworthy's, by a young man aptly named Summer, who died suddenly before he could take responsibility for his child. The whole contrivance, the sending away of the housekeeper to enquire the character of a servant in a distant neighbourhood, the supposed illness of Miss Allworthy in which Jenny nursed her, is unfolded, and the reader, looking back, sees episodes that he saw before, but all in a different light, and bearing new meanings. This discovery is coupled with that of Blifil's having intercepted a letter from his mother on her death-bed to Allworthy, telling him the truth of Tom's parentage. The consequent ruin of Blifil, completed by a letter from Square to Allworthy in which he gives the true explanation of some of the facts

of Tom's behaviour which led to Allworthy's banishment
of him, means of course the reinstatement of Tom in Allworthy's favour, and his consequent acceptance by Squire
Western as the suitor of Sophia.

This is a brief outline of the main threads of the plot.
The whole is supported by innumerable ramifications, all
of which are conducted back to the central thread, and the
reader has the double pleasure of characters pulsating with
spontaneous life, and of a masterly handling of interactions
and surprises that follow each other, symmetrically indeed,
but with a rhythm as natural as the beating of the heart.

As almost every page of this very long novel offers some
fresh evidence of Fielding's powers, illustrations of these
must be partial and random ; but in his profuse, sustained,
inexhaustible flow of characterisation, nothing perhaps is
more remarkable than his delineation of women. That
Fielding was a man who was extremely fond of women is
self-evident ; therefore, what he liked especially in them
were their feminine charms and their feminine virtues.
He legitimately detested termagants, shrews, cold-hearted
women, domineering women, and unattractive women
who tried to enforce men to make love to them. He also
disliked bookish women, female politicians and women of
smart repartee. The type of woman he ardently admired
was beautiful, sensible, modest and tender. Though he must,
in the course of his career, have put up with a good many
who did not fulfil all these requirements, yet his ideal woman
is easy to recognise, and he was one of the few fortunate
men in the world who had his ideal to wife. Where he
shows himself so much in advance of his age is that though
his attitude to women is that of the eminently masculine
man who likes a woman to be thoroughly feminine, he

severely condemned much of the treatment which women received at the hands of society. He compares the wife who is driven to run away from a cruel husband to the hunted hare. " Like that little wretched animal, she pricks up her ears to listen to the voice of her pursuer ; like her, flies away trembling when she hears it, and like her is generally overtaken and destroyed in the end." He exclaims against the wickedness of forced marriage, and of marrying women for their money, which, as he makes Dr. Harrison say in *Amelia*, is " stealing a human creature for her fortune." His condemnation of the double standard of morality by which the woman suffers so much more from an immoral connection than the man has been noticed already in *Jonathan Wild*. In one of his early papers, published in the *Miscellanies*, he inveighs against a state of things which allows men to " enjoy the most delicious fruits" and leave women to endure all the consequent distress.

This fondness for, and sympathy with, women, coupled with his powerful insight, produces some profound studies of female nature which are the subtlest elements of his work.

This penetration however is not called forth by the heroine of *Tom Jones*. Sophia's character, apart from the biographical interest of Fielding's saying that it was founded on his wife's, is singularly attractive, but it is frank and artless. Her sweetness is reflected in the impression she makes on every one she meets with on her journey : landlords, landladies, chambermaids, grooms. Her courage and spirit in running away from a detestable marriage are nobly shown, and also her charming lack of any false pride, when having told Tom she will not consider his proposal for another twelve months, she afterwards consents to be married the next day.

Western, goaded by Allworthy's insisting that she is not

to be over-persuaded, exclaims : " Why, there, you may bid
her unsay it all if you will. Dost repent heartily of thy
promise, dost not, Sophia ? " and Sophia answers, " I do
not repent, nor do I believe I ever shall, of any promise in
favour of Mr. Jones."

Even this lovely creature, whom Fielding can barely
mention without some expression of love, he does not show
entirely without weakness. While her father was violently
urging her to marry Blifil, she was almost tempted to obey,
not only out of fondness for her father, but " when she
reflected how much she herself was to suffer, being indeed
to become little less than a martyr to filial love and duty,
she felt an agreeable tickling in a certain little passion, which
though it bears no immediate affinity either to religion or
virtue, is often so kind as to lend great assistance to executing
the purposes of both."

One of Fielding's very subtle female studies is that of
Jenny Jones, the bookish, plain girl, accused of having a bastard
by Partridge. She bears with exemplary composure all the
jeers and execrations of the village women so long as they
merely abuse her ; she only shows anger when one of them
says that Partridge must have been very hard up to choose so
plain a creature. The gratification of the woman who has
had no sexual success, at being charged with such an escapade,
no less than the ultimate development of Jenny into Mrs.
Waters, an industrious and serious-minded exploiter of
sexual attraction, which, if it develops at all in the intellectual
type, is liable to develop late, is observed with extraordinary
acumen.

More subtle still is the character of Harriet Fitzpatrick,
good and false, sensitive and unscrupulous, cruelly treated
by a hateful husband, but thoroughly unreliable in herself.

She describes to Sophia the agonies of childbirth, rendered even more unendurable when borne for a man one hates. Then, from an object of the deepest compassion, she becomes a pretentious little bore.

" ' How many books do you think I read in three months ? ' ' I can't guess, indeed, cousin,' answered Sophia. ' Perhaps half a score.' ' Half a score ! Half a thousand, child ! ' answered the other. ' I read a good deal in Daniel's *English History of France* ; a great deal in Plutarch's *Lives*, the *Atalantis*, Pope's *Homer*, Dryden's Plays, Chillingworth, the *Countess D'Aulnois*, and Locke's *Human Understanding*.' " Mrs. Fitzpatrick was making her way to London to ask the protection of an Irish peer, whose house, however, she would not visit as his wife was not in town, and she said in the circumstances it would be improper to do so. At the end of the book we are told :

" Mrs. Fitzpatrick is separated from her husband and retains the little remains of her fortune. She lives in reputation at the polite end of the town, and is so good an economist that she spends three times the income of her fortune without running into debt."

The book throughout its course throws out a profusion of characters and episodes, any one of which makes a study. We say : " Here is God's plenty." Besides these, there is a perpetual flow of observations ; these vary from those of the gravest kind, such as the comment on the gypsies' happiness under their autocratic rules—" In reality I know of but one solid objection to absolute monarchy. The only defect in which excellent constitution seems to be the difficulty of finding any man adequate to the office of an absolute monarch." (Bk. XII, Chap. XII.)—to those which, telling us about the follies of Fielding's age, show us how like they were to our own—"Jones now declared that they must certainly have lost their way; but this, the guide insisted upon, was impossible; a word which, in common conversation, is often used to signify not only improbable, but often what is really very likely, and sometimes what hath certainly happened; an hyperbolical violence like that which is so frequently offered to the words infinite and eternal; by the former of which it is usual to express a distance of half a yard, and by the latter a duration of five minutes." (Bk. XII, Chap. XI.)

The master-observer, and especially he who observes through the lens of a comic vision, is himself too much detached to exert a hypnotic influence on his readers, however deeply he may interest them. Richardson is a spell-binder, Fielding is not. It is possible, when reading parts of *Clarissa*, to feel that this is the greatest novel in the language. When the volume is shut, judgment and common sense come stealing back. It is interesting to notice that the novelists whom we may call spell-binders, have usually been people of unbalanced temperament: Richardson, Dickens, Charlotte Brontë are examples. Fielding's was not the temperament to produce the hypnotic effect; at the same time, it must be said that his observation of mankind was gained through experience. He says too (Preface, Bk. IX): "No man can paint a distress well which he doth not feel while he is painting it . . . in the same manner it is with the ridiculous. I am convinced I never make my reader laugh heartily but where I have laughed before him."

Tom Jones is unique, because it is not only in itself one of the first and one of the greatest English novels; it also contains a statement of Fielding's theory of how the novel should be written. This is found, *passim*, in the prefaces to the eighteen books into which *Tom Jones* is divided. For those who feel a personal fondness for Fielding, these prefaces are even more fascinating than the story. In the latter, his great powers are used consciously to describe the characters of his imagination. In the prefaces, they are used unconsciously to reveal his own.

Fielding has, with great justice, been called the Father of the English Novel, and his extraordinarily well-balanced temperament presents the two aspects, very rarely found together, of great imagination and great critical power. A novel of this rank, which contains such a dissertation on the art of novel-writing, indicates a mind of the most unusual capacity.

Fielding knew himself to be an innovator ; in Book II he says, in speaking of his time-scheme, which will now pass over years, and now descend to the minutiæ of days : " as I am, in reality, the founder of a new province in writing, so I am at liberty to make what laws I please therein. And these laws my readers, whom I consider as my subjects, are bound to believe in and obey." Scott said (in his preface to *The Fortunes of Nigel*) that " Smollett, Le Sage and others, emancipating themselves from the strictness of the rules he has laid down, have written a history of miscellaneous adventures which befall an individual in the course of life, rather than the plot of a regular and connected epopeia, where every step brings us a point nearer to the final catastrophe." The only novelist who thoroughly carries out Fielding's conception of plot, in which every incident bears upon the rest, is Jane Austen.

Fielding, as Scott said, had " high notions of the dignity of an art which he may be considered as having founded," and he puts the critic in his proper place. He points out

(Bk. V) that whereas the critic's original function was to *deduce* the laws of an art from the masterpieces already accomplished, modern critics " now have the assurance to give laws to those authors from whose predecessors they originally received them."

The prefaces abound in remarks on the qualifications a novel-writer must possess, as where he says of himself : " We . . . who are admitted behind the scenes of this great theatre of nature (and no author ought to write anything besides dictionaries and spelling books who hath not this privilege) "—but his most important passages are found in Books IX and XIII. In the former, speaking " of those who lawfully may, and of those who may not, write such histories as this," he says that three essential qualities in the novelist are : genius, learning and experience of human nature. "Genius alone," he says, "is not sufficient without a good share of learning . . . nature can only furnish us with capacity . . . learning must contribute part at least of the materials."

What counsels of perfection ! It scarcely matters that there have been few, besides Fielding himself, at any time, capable of fulfilling them, and that there are none now. Nor is the value of what he says greatly impaired by the fact that not good novels only, but great novels, have been written, of which the authors could not boast all the equipment he says is absolutely necessary. As a code of rules for the writing of novels, his remarks contain more practical guidance and good sense than anyone else has so far provided, and his conception of the dignity of the art of novel-writing is something on which our generation looks back, as upon some lofty range of mountains on the sky-line.

In the preface to Book XIII, he invokes the " bright love

of fame " and cries : " Comfort me by a solemn assurance
that when the little parlour in which I sit at this instant shall
be reduced to a worse-furnished box, I shall be read with
honour by those who never knew nor saw me, and whom
I shall neither know nor see." The comfort should have
been given, for the assurance was to be most thoroughly
fulfilled. Gibbon mistakenly supposed Fielding's family
to be descended from the Hapsburgs, but the error does not
affect the splendid panegyric he pronounced upon *Tom
Jones*, of which he said : " That exquisite picture of human
manners will outlive the palace of the Escurial and the
imperial eagle of the house of Austria."

Two things are known of Fielding while he was composing
Tom Jones. He spent part of the time at Tiverton, outside
Bath (where he was probably taking the waters), and while
here he dined daily with Allen at Prior Park. Allen was one
of the most excellent examples of what the enlightened patron
could be. He had sent Fielding two hundred pounds before
he knew him. When one reads of Prior Park one cannot
but remember the description of Allworthy's hospitality,
the tact and good breeding with which the guests, while
warmly welcomed, were allowed to go their own way, with
no suggestion that the host had a claim on their talents and
conversation in return for their dinner.

The other anecdote is that of a house-party at Mr. Saunder-
son-Miller's, of Radway in Warwickshire. Lord Chatham
was one of the guests and the party was further remarkable
because Fielding was there and read some of *Tom Jones*
aloud to the company.

Fielding says in his dedication to Lyttelton that the latter
had suggested the plan of the novel to him, and that " I
partly owe to you my existence during great part of the time

I have employed in composing it." For how long and to what extent Lyttelton had supported him is unknown. Fielding says in the preface : " I here present you with the labours of some years of my life." The only other detail we learn about the writing of the book is that he sometimes had to keep his children quiet when he was working on it. In the famous preface to the thirteenth book, he asks that the novel's success may bring a provision for " the prattling babes whose innocent play hath often been interrupted by my labours."

Andrew Millar paid him six hundred pounds for the work, and then, finding it sell so well, added another hundred.

Of contemporary opinion of the book it is difficult to form a general estimate. It was extremely popular, and two of Richardson's " ladies," the Misses Hill, committed the *faux pas* of telling him young ladies everywhere now called their lovers their " Tom Jones," and gentlemen spoke ot their " Sophias." Though the book was undoubtedly one of the most admired and famous novels of the century, it nevertheless aroused some surprising criticism, which usually takes two well-defined lines. One, that the young hero's immorality is disgusting to the virtuous, and the other that so many of the characters are drawn from low life, they can have no interest for the polite.

Most of the unfavourable criticism of Fielding is not worth repeating, but one example must be mentioned, not for its intrinsic merit but for its source. When Boswell praised the author of *Tom Jones*, Dr. Johnson exclaimed : " He was a blockhead." When Boswell expressed astonishment at " so strange an assertion," Johnson amplified the statement but left it even obscurer than before. " What I mean by his being a blockhead is that he was a barren rascal." Professor

Saintsbury has given the probable explanation of Johnson's
extraordinary attitude, that Johnson himself struggled very
hard to keep his amorous propensities in check, and he was
goaded by Fielding's gay, care-free attitude to sexual pleasure.
The remark remains an awe-inspiring example of how utterly
irresponsible a great man's prejudice will allow him to be.

The question of immorality as applied to either Fielding
or Richardson is at best irrelevant ; but the decrying of
Fielding on this account at the same time that Richardson
was exalted with such religious fervour, not as an artist
only but as a moralist, tempts one to ask : if the standard
of morality is to be applied to these great writers, which of
them has the healthy attitude to sex ? The author who treats
of it frankly and openly but without detail or suggestiveness,
or the one who through two lengthy novels keeps the reader's
imagination in a long, drawn out suspense, culminating in
a wedding night and a rape respectively ? The argument
that in *Tom Jones* it is the hero who is guilty of immorality,
while in *Clarissa* it is the villain, seems almost too dis-
ingenuous. If a novel be replete with lewd excitement,
as *Clarissa* is, what does it matter on whose account it is
introduced ? If the faculties of such readers as Mrs. Chapone
were so alive to impropriety in Fielding, what, one wonders,
bemused them when their owners were reading the letters
of Mr. Lovelace to Mr. Belford ? Irritating as we find
the prudery of the nineteenth century, it had at least the
merit of consistency. It bowdlerised Fielding and Richardson impartially. Every century has its own peculiar dis-
tortions, the twentieth no less than the eighteenth, but our
sympathies in sexual matters are much nearer to Fielding's
than were many of his contemporaries.

The True Patriot, which had been inspired by the '45

Rebellion, lost its impetus as an occasional production after the Pretender's defeat, and was replaced by another paper, anti-Jacobite but of more general interest, *The Jacobite's Journal*. But Fielding had not for long the leisure to keep it up. In 1749 he received his one really important piece of preferment, and was appointed J.P. for Middlesex.

To be eligible for this appointment, it was necessary for him to have a property qualification ; the Duke of Bedford (whose kindness to him Fielding had already acknowledged in the introduction to *Tom Jones*) allowed him to rent a house in Bow Street on favourable terms, and here Fielding's short but momentous life as a justice was lived out.

Fielding's great success as a magistrate and his remarkable contribution to society in this capacity would be better known if it had not been eclipsed by his success as a novelist. In the first place, he gained the confidence and applause of his colleagues. He was chosen Chairman of the Session in Hick's Hall, and as such delivered a Charge to the Westminster Grand Jury, June 1749. This was so highly thought of that it was published " at the unanimous request of the Gentlemen of the Grand Jury." In its concluding passages, Fielding showed with what an eagle eye he viewed his scope. " Grand jurors, gentlemen," he said, " are in reality the only censors of the nation. As such the manners of the people are in your hands and in yours only."

Fielding was unusually well qualified to be a magistrate, always an exacting role but in his day even more so than now, because the poverty that begets crime was then infinitely greater than it is to-day. He was assisted by his brother John, and had the services of an excellent clerk called Brogden. Mr. C. B. Jones has pointed out that Fielding never satirises counsels or advocates, only solicitors, attorneys, magistrates, constables, bailiffs and watchmen. But the vigour and consistency with which he holds these officials up to censure and ridicule give an alarming picture of the general standard of efficiency and probity with which the law was administered everywhere except in the law courts. His two main accusations are : gross ignorance of the law and shameless corruption. That these two drawbacks were, on his appointment, instantly banished from the court in Bow Street, makes one understand how he immediately acquired the reputation he did of phenomenal honesty and competence. Smollett wrote a pamphlet against him, *Habbakuk Hilding, Justice and Chapman*, accusing him of filthy personal habits and of being off his head ; this tells us a good deal about Smollett, but nothing about Fielding. The term " trading justice " arose from the fact that part of the justice's salary was taken from fines imposed in court, and Fielding said that " by composing instead of inflaming the quarrels of porters and beggars (which I blush when I say hath not been universally practised) and by refusing to take a shilling from a man who most undoubtedly would not have had another left, I had reduced an income of about £500 a year of the dirtiest money upon earth to little more than £300, a considerable proportion of which remained with my clerk."

Horace Walpole disliked Fielding because of the latter's enmity to his father. It is he who has left the account of two of his friends Rigby and Bathurst calling at Bow Street to give a servant in charge. It was night ; Fielding kept no hours, and lived above his court room, but he said they must come next morning. The party refused to wait, went upstairs and broke into his parlour " where they found him," says Walpole " banqueting with a blind man, a whore and three Irishmen on some cold mutton and a bone of ham both in one dish and the dirtiest cloth." When it is realised that the blind man was John Fielding and the female companion the second Mrs. Fielding, one feels that Horace Walpole deserved a rebuke in the words of Johnson : " Do not tell that story again, sir. You cannot conceive how poor a figure you make in the telling of it."

Fielding during his tenure of office produced a tract of great importance, which had an immediate influence on the legislature. This was : *An Inquiry into the Cause of the late increase of Robbers*, 1751. He ascribed this epidemic of crime to four main causes : a mania for dissipation which had now reached the lower orders and was catered for, and encouraged, by a great number of disreputable places of amusement ; the prevalence of gambling ; the fact that people were so anxious to retrieve their stolen property that they advertised for its return " and no questions asked," thus defeating the efforts of the law, and, most productive of all, the widespread curse of gin-drinking. A few weeks after the publication of Fielding's pamphlet, Hogarth brought out his ghastly plate : " Gin Lane," and two months after Fielding's publication, the Tippling Act was passed, which imposed certain restrictions on the sale of spirits. When one remembers that the penalty for the theft of any article over the value of five shillings was death, one gains some idea of the ocean[1] of violent crime and retributive, crime-begetting violence through which Fielding bore his manful way, holding out like a beacon an ideal of justice and humanity, some principles of which would be regarded as ideal even at the present day. That he was frequently, by our standards, harsh, goes

---

[1] Fielding speaks in the *Inquiry* of " many cartloads of our fellow-creatures . . once in six weeks . . . carried to slaughter."

without saying. We think a rogue should be psycho-analysed, and Fielding thought he should be hanged. But apart from many suggestions for practical administration, his great contribution to society was the recognition that you cannot do away with crime until you have done away with the causes of crime, and his clear statement that poverty, overcrowding, and unemployment when a man is willing to work, " and that, in a nation of such trade and opulence," will bring a retribution on the rest of the community in violence, theft and murder.

The legal remedies he suggested for the punishment of crime were more speedily acted upon than his suggestions for preventing it ; but it is a tribute to his great influence that two more Acts are ascribed to it, in 1752—an Act for the better preventing Thefts and Robberies, and an Act for the better preventing the Horrid Crime of Murder.

Fielding's powers of mind were apparently inexhaustible. Despite the cares and exertions of his office, he found energy to write a novel. In 1751, he published *Amelia*.

Tom Jones has all the accumulated experience and the weight of Fielding's forty-two years behind it. *Amelia*, published only two years later, is a book of entirely different scope. It is a picture of the first few years, marked by every kind of misfortune and distress, of an exceptionally happy marriage.

Lady Bute said that Amelia was a portrait of the first Mrs. Fielding, and that it did her no more than justice ; that Fielding had drawn himself in Captain Booth, and that she was persuaded many of the incidents in the story were drawn from life. She cited that of Amelia's broken nose which she got through being tipped out of a chaise, an accident which had happened to Charlotte Fielding. The realism which inspired Fielding to give a heroine a broken nose, was unacceptable to contemporary readers. Richardson spoke sneeringly of the beauty " without a nose," and Johnson said " that vile broken nose, never cured," injured the popularity of the book. Fielding perhaps found that the disfigurement conjured up was more than he had meant to suggest. In a subsequent edition he added the sentence : " She was indeed a most charming woman, and I know not whether the little scar on her nose did not rather add to than diminish her beauty." Whatever the extent of this injury in Mrs. Fielding, it had not lessened her husband's passionate admiration of her beauty.

There is no " set piece " of description of Amelia as there is of Sophia, but her beauty is much more vividly suggested. A heroine in Sophia's situation is expected to be beautiful, and having received from Fielding " a short hint of what we can do in the sublime, and a description of Miss Sophia Western," the reader is prepared to let his imagination do the rest. Amelia is the harassed wife and mother, with a husband constantly in prison for debt, her time taken up with cooking and taking care of her children, reduced to pawning her gowns and, when the servant has stolen her shifts, left without a clean one to put on. In these circumstances, her great beauty comes before the reader as a constant delight. Whiteness is a conventional attribute of beauty, but we feel that Fielding really was describing a woman with a very white skin ; he not only speaks of " her snowy arms," but he says that, when frightened, " Amelia turned as white as snow." " Vermillion " is the colour brought into her cheeks by exercise or gaiety. When her eyes shone with delight, he says that in the words of Horace, they were too dazzling to be looked at. When she brings her children home from a delightful party where they have been given presents, she is " all a blaze of beauty."

The marriage at the time of the book has lasted some years, but Booth still speaks to his wife as " My lovely angel," and when their evening guests have gone and they go to bed, Fielding says : " They retired into each other's arms." Booth, discussing love with the womaniser Colonel James, says : " With regard to love, I declare I have never found anything cloying in it. I have lived almost alone with my wife near three years together, was never tired of her company nor ever wished for any other."

The picture of married tenderness is wonderfully drawn. Booth says that he supported his wife in his arms while she was in labour, and made her caudle with his own hands. The most celebrated passage in this book is that in which Amelia makes a dish of hashed mutton for his supper, and though she herself feels the need of a drink, denies herself half a pint of wine to save sixpence, " while her husband was paying a debt of several guineas, incurred by the ace of trumps being in the hands of his adversary." Fielding's descriptions of children are exquisite : there is Parson Adams's little Dick, who, when his sister says she would not give Fanny a half-penny if she were starving, cries : " Indeed but I would, and, father, rather than poor Fanny shall be starved, I will give her all this bread and cheese (offering what he held in his hand)" ; the description of Tom as a baby asleep in All-worthy's bed, and all the pictures of Amelia's children ; from the parents' first visit to their baby at nurse, when " we made words and meanings out of every sound," to the occasion of the family's walking in Hyde Park with Amelia's foster-brother, Sergeant Atkinson. Amelia, feeling faint, walks on with her husband while Atkinson tries to bring the children after. "He offered his hand to Miss, who refused it and burst into tears." Booth has to resign his wife to Atkinson and bring the children himself.

The weak part of the design is Captain Booth himself. Lady Bute said he was a self-portrait and to a point this is obviously true. Booth's improvidence, his cheerfulness, his devotion to his wife and children in spite of his allowing himself to be seduced by another woman, are easily recognised, as also is the description of his appearance by the jealous Colonel James, who declares that Booth has the shoulders of a drayman, the legs of a chairman, and a nose like the proboscis of an elephant—a good caricature of the long, straight nose that continues the line of the forehead in Hogarth's portrait. But though Booth has Fielding's appearance and his weaknesses, he has none of his strength. When Booth laments to his wife that instead of marrying him, she should have made a great match such as her beauty and fortune entitled her to, and Amelia replies, "I might have been great, but I could never have been happy with another man," we feel that these words were actually spoken, but that they were spoken to a man very different from Captain Booth.

The story of *Amelia* is entirely domestic and though in retrospect the early scenes of the marriage are given, which include the run-away match of the heiress, a period of service in Gibraltar and a short, idyllic spell of living in the country as a yeoman farmer, the action of the book, unlike that of its two predecessors, takes place entirely in London, between the dismal scenes of Newgate, Booth's humble lodgings, the houses of the great in Grosvenor Square, Vauxhall, Hyde Park, the Mall, Birdcage Walk, the pawn shop of Monmouth Street and the bailiff's lock-up in Gray's Inn Lane.

The opening scene is the most powerful in the book—
the picture of Newgate to which Booth has been consigned
on an entire misunderstanding by Justice Thrasher, of whom
Fielding observes : " I own I have been sometimes inclined
to think that this office of a justice of peace requires some
knowledge of the law, for this simple reason : because
in every case which comes before him, he is to judge and
act according to the law.   Again, as these laws are contained
in a great variety of books (the statutes which relate to a justice
of peace making of themselves at least two large volumes in
folio, and that part of his jurisdiction which is founded on
the common law being dispersed in above a hundred
volumes), I cannot conceive how this knowledge should be
acquired without reading ; and yet, certain it is, Mr. Thrasher
never read one syllable of the matter."

The scene of Booth's commitment, his arrival in the
gaol, the poverty and misery spread around, the wretched
or ferocious inmates, makes a part of that grim background
against which Amelia herself glows with her luminous
warmth.

In the gaol, the one being who is well fed, well dressed
and has money to spare, is the beautiful but fierce Miss
Matthews, committed for the murder of her betrayer (though
he recovers from his wound and she is therefore released).
Miss Matthews is an old acquaintance and she discloses to
Booth that she has always loved him.   Booth's appalling
situation in the Newgate of 1750 makes it natural for him
to welcome the advances of a clean, beautiful, elegant woman,
whose high spirit is proof against the horrors of the place
and whose money can buy wine, food and privacy inside it.
Miss Matthews however is as a tiger cat who has tasted blood,
and after his release Booth is tormented by her threats that

unless he comes to visit her she will expose him to his wife. In one of the finest scenes of the book, Booth finally confesses to Amelia his brief amour inside the prison ; Amelia then produces from her pocket a letter from Miss Matthews in which she has already betrayed him, but which Amelia has not only decided to overlook, but has actually forgotten, in the pressure of their domestic troubles.

The other characters of the story are all connected with it through Amelia who is the inspiration of the whole book. The wealthy, dissolute Colonel James marries her friend, Miss Bath, but tiring of her, begins to lay siege to Amelia. The Booths find lodgings with a substantial friendly, good-natured Mrs. Ellison, through whom Amelia becomes acquainted with a reserved young widow, Mrs. Bennet, whom she takes to very much. Mrs. Ellison kindly takes Amelia to an oratorio, to which they arrive so early that they have a long wait before they see " the back of Mr. Handel." But the tedium is relieved by another early-comer, a gentle-man in a rug coat, wearing a patch over his eye, who politely buys Amelia a copy of the score and holds a wax candle by which she studies it.

Mrs. Ellison presently introduces to the Booths a cousin of hers, "My Lord," a wealthy and extremely affable young man, who wears richly embroidered clothes. His condescension is astonishing. He offers his influence to get Booth the command of a company and pays particular attention to Amelia's children ; it is from a day at his house that Amelia and her " little things " return, loaded with trinkets. Booth's uneasiness is alternately alarmed and soothed, until Mrs. Ellison, in the presence of Mrs. Bennet, offers Amelia a masquerade ticket. Mrs. Bennet now takes the first oppor-tunity of telling Amelia her own story, of how, as a bride, she had come to London with her husband, a clergyman looking for preferment, and the hideous account of her seduction by "My Lord," her contracting his venereal disease, and infecting her husband ; of her husband's death from a heart attack, and of Mrs. Ellison's contemptuous good nature in securing from My Lord a pension for her of £150 a year. Fielding's skill as a story-teller, which is not so much in evidence in this novel, suddenly reveals itself when Mrs. Bennet, at the end of her story, says how she first met My Lord. It was at the Oratorio she said. She had been taken there much too early by a friend who was one of his procuresses, and he was sitting, the only occupant of the gallery, wearing a rug coat with a patch over his eye.

The character of My Lord is the more sinister for being anonymous. His name is never mentioned. When a character has taken hold of the reader's imagination as really frightening, everything connected with it seems a fresh source of alarm, and the extravagantly embroidered clothes in which My Lord always appears heighten the repulsiveness of his effect. Mrs. Bennet's story of how, while he courted her, he sat with her six-months-old baby on his lap, letting it drink tea, and not minding how the tea was spilt over his embroidery, is peculiarly horrible. The end of this prodigious womaniser, who would spend endless time and money in securing a new woman but never had her more than once, is that " he became at last so rotten that he stank above ground." There is so much in the book that is grim and indeed ghastly, that the strength of the beautiful passages may be judged from the fact that it is they and not the rest that give its distinguishing character to the whole.

The happy conclusion is brought about by the discovery that Amelia is, after all, her mother's heiress, and had been defrauded up till now by her malignant sister. (The fact that one of Charlotte Cradock's sisters was cut off with a shilling in the mother's will, the small fortune going entirely to Charlotte, suggests that this may be some form of another piece of autobiography.) The happy and now fortunate Booths retire to their house in the country, where their neighbour is the good Dr. Harrison who had originally supported Booth's courtship.

Fielding said (*Covent Garden Journal*) that of all his progeny, Amelia was his favourite child. If he meant the character, " this poor girl," his taste was natural enough. As a novel, few people would consider it the equal of either *Joseph Andrews* or *Tom Jones*, though it was the favourite of Johnson, who paid it the compliment of reading it through at a sitting. Apart from Amelia herself, it lacks the light and buoyancy, the wonderful stimulus of the two earlier books. At the same time, it has qualities which Fielding never surpassed else-where. His attitude to the people in the book, of insight and tolerance, recalls Murphy's remark about him in real life, that : " it is to the honour of those whom he loved that he had too much penetration to be deceived in their characters." He shows that mixture of bad and good, which we take for granted in real life but do not expect to find shown with such remorseless clarity in fiction. There is the ridiculous Colonel Bath with his touchiness and his murderous notions of " honour " who when Booth, a very courageous man, said he did not want to fight a duel with his best friend, " grinned horribly a ghastly smile, or rather sneer," who, yet, when his sister was ill, was found by Booth, wrapped up in a woman's bed-gown and a dirty flannel night-cap, warming her posset over an expiring fire. There is Mrs. Ellison, the friendly, sensible, good-natured landlady, who

7

turns out to be a pimp for My Lord; Amelia's friend who,
as Miss Bath, had been a true friend to her, but as the wealthy
Mrs. James, felt obliged, until melted by Amelia's sweetness, to behave to her with the airs of a lady of fashion. There
is the young, gentle, well-educated, much-tried Mrs. Bennet,
who drinks secretly and keeps a bottle of brandy in her bedroom, becoming quarrelsome when she has taken too much,
and the good Dr. Harrison himself, who is susceptible to
flattery. The triumph of Amelia's own character is that it
appears to be without faults and yet never seems unnatural or
inhuman. The story of her early married life is a wonderful
dwelling within memory and imagination. Fielding's view
of the external world had always been exceptionally clear-
sighted, but the stinging vigour of his early attack had im-
parted a kind of gaiety, even to the blackest scenes of *Jonathan
Wild*. In *Amelia*, his spirit as he looks at the rest of the world,
has lost its extraordinary animation. The wretchedness
that has come under the eye of the humane and elderly
magistrate, is treated in a different key from that of the earlier
satires. But in the picture of Amelia herself, the old animation is all there. There is no hint that she was really dead,
and that when she had died, he had nearly lost his reason.
In this act of creation, " Time remembered is grief forgotten."

Amelia is now by general consent thought the least brilliant
of Fielding's three novels, but in the author's life-time it
sold the best. Andrew Millar paid a thousand guineas for the
copyright, and Johnson says a second edition was called for
on the first day of publication.

In the following year, Fielding embarked on his last
piece of journalism. This was the *Covent Garden Journal*
and of all the collected essays given by Murphy from *The*

Champion, The True Patriot, The Jacobite's Journal and *The Covent Garden Journal*, those from the latter make the best reading. They contain, *inter alia*, the germ of Thackeray's "Yellow plush" language, in No. 8, a skit on the Robin Hood Society, in the form of a debate : " Whether relidgin was of any youse to a sosyaty ? " in which Mr. Skotchum the barber said : " Sir, I ham of opinion, that relidgin can be of no youse to any mortal sole ; bycause as why, relidgin is of no youse to trayd, and if relidgin is of no youse to trayd, how is it youseful to sosyaty ? " There is the fascinating *Modern Glossary*, with such definitions as :

NO-BODY. All the people in Great Britain except about 1200.

ROGUE ⎫
RASCAL ⎭ A man of a different party from yourself.

Best of all, it contains (No. 33) a description of Fielding " travelling westward " the previous summer, and breakfasting in the kitchen of a Somersetshire inn in the early summer morning, admiring the exquisite view of river, fields and woods, in such delight " as made me thank heaven I was born." This delicious tranquillity is broken by " a genteel whistle and the noise of a pair of slippers descending the staircase." A young man bursts in, loud, bumptious, overbearing, swearing at every other word, insulting the patient innkeeper and playing off the airs of a man-about-town on the simple rustics. Some months afterwards, Fielding says that he recognised this young fellow in London, behind the counter of a linen-draper's shop.

In 1753, he published a work which had cost him much thought and labour, but which, whatever interest it may have aroused, bore no practical result. This was *A Proposal for making effective provision for the Poor*. The scheme was on the lines of a community including hostels, workshops, infirmaries and prisons. That it savours too much of a penal settlement for many whose only crime was poverty, will be forcibly felt in this age. At the same time, the scheme contained much humanity and much common sense, and as a constructive attempt to mitigate great evils, it showed yet again that Fielding's social conscience was much in advance of the standards of his own time.

In the same year, Fielding published *A Clear State of the Case of Elizabeth Canning*, an account of the astonishing case of the girl who declared she had been kidnapped by gipsies and imprisoned in a house on the Hertford Road for four weeks. Fielding, before whom the case was originally heard, was among those who thought Elizabeth Canning was telling the truth, and an old gipsy woman, Mary Squire, was sentenced to death. The Lord Mayor, however, instigated an appeal against this verdict and Squire was released, Elizabeth Canning herself being subsequently charged with perjury and sentenced to transportation. The case aroused a ferment of interest and the whole truth of it has never been discovered. It is generally supposed that Fielding was mistaken in his view of it. The business has this further interest, that a print was circulated, of Fielding holding Elizabeth Canning by the hand and confronting the gipsies and their supporters. This drawing of him, tall, emaciated and with bandaged legs, but unquestionably the dominating figure of the scene, is the only likeness of him that is known to have been made during his lifetime. Hogarth's drawing of him, made from memory, was however said by his friends to be an excellent likeness of him as they last saw him. It shows a long, grecian nose, deep-set black eyes, a pronounced chin and a mouth fallen in from loss of teeth. Formidable, high-spirited, humorous, the drawing has the air of a speaking likeness.

Fielding was now so ill with what he calls "a lingering, imperfect gout," that he sent to engage lodgings in Bath. Before he could get there, he was sent for by the Duke of Newcastle, and asked to draw up some plan to control the robber gangs, who had been responsible for five murders in one week, and were terrorising London. Fielding, as he had shown in *Jonathan Wild*, had a knowledge of the inner workings of such gangs. Ill as he was, he threw himself into the drafting of a plan, which the Privy Council adopted, and with such success that, he said, a day or two after he received the necessary moneys to pay the thief-taker, the robbers were broken up, "seven of them were in actual custody, and the rest driven, some out of town, and others out of the kingdom." During November and December 1753, usually the peak months for these outrages, not a single murder or robbery was reported.

But he himself was now at death's door, with a complication of gout, asthma, jaundice and dropsy. He retired to a small house he had acquired at Fordhook, Ealing. His family here were his wife, with the three surviving of her five children, William aged six, Sophia aged four, and the baby, Allen, who was born in April 1754. There was, besides a daughter of his first marriage, Harriet, who would have been some years under twenty.

Having been told that he must not face another English winter, he decided to go for a time to Portugal. His wife and Harriet were to go with him, and two servants, a maid and man.

The Journal of a Voyage to Lisbon, with which he beguiled his inactive hours on board ship, tells in its introductory

pages of his fatigues in the long examinations of the robbers
that had exhausted his remaining strength, of his dire sickness, and the remedies that were tried for it, and how he
spent the last morning in his home.

"Wednesday, June 26, 1754. On this day, the most
melancholy sun I ever beheld arose, and found me awake
at my house at Fordhook. By the light of this sun I was, in
my own opinion, last to behold and take leave of some of
those creatures, on whom I doated with a mother-like
fondness. . . . As I could not conquer nature, I submitted
entirely to her, and . . . under pretence of giving me leave
to enjoy, she drew me to suffer the company of my little
ones, during eight hours. And I doubt not whether in that
time I did not undergo more than in all my distemper."

The *Journal of a Voyage to Lisbon* is one of the most charming things of its kind ever written. It has not only the
fascination for the modern reader of giving him, almost with
a sense of clairvoyance, a complete impression of all the
experiences undergone in being taken on board at Rotherhithe and enduring the voyage to the Tagus in a British
vessel of 1754 ; Fielding's peculiar gift of observation which
is at once objective, sympathetic and informed, provides
this material; the book has also the indescribable charm of
his own personality. No circumstances could have provided
a better mirror for his mind than its being turned in upon
itself in a sea-voyage, when the sea-sickness of his wife and
daughter and the preoccupation of the captain gave him
hours of solitude, such as he had never endured before and
hated now.

When he arrived at Rotherhithe he had to be carried on
board, and emaciated, ghastly pale and helpless as he was,
rows of sailors through whom he passed, laughed, insulted

and jeered at his appearance. The indignation he felt was
not altogether a personal one. It was aroused, he said, by
" a lively picture of that cruelty and inhumanity in the nature
of men which I have often contemplated with concern, and
which leads the mind into a train of very melancholy and
uncomfortable thoughts." [1]

After so unfortunate a beginning, and despite the annoy-
ance of repeated delays which made it necessary for him to
be tapped again for the dropsy, while the Captain waited
upon the wind, Fielding's natural cheerfulness, and his powers
of enjoyment showed themselves as much his friend as ever.
As they passed along the coast of Kent, his heart stirred with
delight at the sight of the shipping ; he wondered that this
part of the coast was not more often chosen for building than
Middlesex and Surrey, since from it people would enjoy
" viewing a succession of ships, with all their sails expanded
to the winds, bounding over the waves." And he thought
it a pity that so great a pleasure was neglected as that of
" sailing ourselves in little vessels of our own." He would
have been a keen yachtsman.

He was delighted, when, off the Devonshire coast, they
procured " very fine clouted cream and fresh bread and
butter from the shore," on which they all made " a very
cheerful breakfast." Here too, he included a panegyric
on the delicious cyder of Mr. Giles Leverance of Cheeshurst
near Dartmouth, of which he bought a hogshead to take
to Lisbon and two hogsheads to send to friends on shore, for
a price of five pounds ten shillings. Before they left the
Channel, several fishing boats went to them with fish, and
as a man accustomed to the stale wares and extortionate

[1] Ten years ago, one might have said that humanity had become more
civilised since Fielding's time. We may say at least that English sailors have.

rates of the London fishmongers, Fielding could scarcely contain his astonishment at the excellence and cheapness of the fresh-caught fish, " very large soals at fourpence a pair—and whiting, of almost a preposterous size, at ninepence a score."

Fielding had been a huntsman in his youth and he would not have understood a sentimental reluctance to shooting or fishing, but his humane nature, so much in advance of its age, was grieved by one of the sailors' attempting to harpoon a rock-fish, from which " the poor wretch escaped to linger out a few hours, with probably great torments."

His wife's absolute devotion to him and to his comfort is revealed in almost everything he says about her, and so too, is his grateful dependence on her   Her heroic common sense rescued the party at Ryde from all the discomforts inflicted on them by the landlady, Mrs. Francis, by the unconventional step of ordering dinner to be served in a barn, " dry, warm, oaken-floored," " opening at one end on a green field and a beautiful prospect." Here they dined on beans and bacon, soles and lobsters, " with more appetite, more real, solid luxury and more festivity than was ever seen in an entertainment at White's."

When an attack of agonising toothache at last allowed Mrs. Fielding to sleep, he says the circumstance would have given him some happiness, " could I have known how to supply those spirits that were raised by it," but unfortunately he was left " in a disposition of enjoying an agreeable hour without the assistance of a companion, which has always appeared to me necessary to such enjoyment." We can appreciate from this, the mutual unselfishness of the two, when, the ship being forced to drop anchor at Ryde once more, he says : " I persuaded my wife, whom it was no easy matter for me to force from my side, to take a walk on shore." The most touching tribute to Mrs. Fielding and to his daughter is paid when he says that, during a raging storm, when the threat of drowning was imminent : " My dear wife and child must pardon me, if what I did not conceive to be any great evil to myself, I was not much terrified with the thoughts of happening to them ; in truth I have often thought they are both too good, and too gentle, to be trusted to the power of any man I know, to whom they could possibly be so trusted."

The observation, and the power of describing what he saw, that had peopled the coaches and inns of *Joseph Andrews* and *Tom Jones,* had not deserted him, dying though he was. The master of the *Queen of Portugal,* Captain Richard Veal, who had begun his seafaring life as a privateer, is a figure of inimitable contrasts and consistency, and to compare him with the captains in *Roderick Random* is to see the difference between Smollett's temper and Fielding's in a nut-shell. Veal dressed himself in a red coat, a cockaded hat and a sword when he went on shore. He was harsh and unscrupulous in discharging his obligations to his passengers, but " acted the part of a father to his sailors," expressing " great tenderness for any of them when ill," and howled with grief when his favourite kitten was found smothered under a feather-bed. He had a serious difference of opinion with Fielding, when the mate burst into the cabin where Fielding was sitting with his wife after dinner and disturbed them by starting to stow away half a hogshead of beer in bottles. Fielding asked him to wait till a more convenient time, when the Captain, summoned by his mate to the scene, attempted to override his passenger in a blustering and abusive manner. Fielding for once appears absolutely to have lost his temper. He threatened to leave the ship and to sue the

Captain for breach of contract. The name of the Law was
so dreadful to Captain Veal that he went down on his knee
to ask pardon. Fielding says : " I did not suffer a brave man
and an old man to remain a moment in this posture ; but
I immediately forgave him . . . neither did the greatness of
my mind dictate, nor the force of my Christianity exact this
forgiveness . . . I forgave him from a motive which would
make men much more forgiving if they were much wiser
than they are ; because it was convenient for me to do so."

Mr. and Mrs. Francis, the supine innkeeper of Ryde and
his termagant wife, read like something out of the novels
themselves. When Mrs. Francis, a perfect prodigy of the
mean and disobliging, first refuses to produce anything for
the visitors' comfort, and then, when her fantastic charges are
met without demur, grumbles that " she knew not how it
was that others got their money by gentlefolks, but for her
part she had not the art of it," we realise, if we did not
before, how little exaggeration has gone to the making of
Mrs. Tow-wouse and the landlady of the inn at Upton.
We believe Fielding when he says : " I have writ little more
than I have seen."

It was not the observer of manners only who was on
board the *Queen of Portugal*, but the zealous, reforming
magistrate. Throughout the voyage, he is alive to incom-
petence and abuses. At Rotherhithe, he gives a mordant
picture of bureaucracy, in the overbearing insolence of
the customs officers who burst into the cabin where he and
his wife are sitting. Mr. Austin Dobson suggests that Mary
Daniel's humble origin made Fielding the more vigilant
to see that every due respect was paid to her, and that some
of the sharpness with which he rebuked the blustering louts
was owing to this. Having made the foremost man remove

his hat as a gesture, Fielding then said he dared say the lady would allow him to put it on again, but the man's surliness " failed not to convince me that if I should condescend to become more gentle, he would soon grow more rude."

His acquaintance with sailors had hitherto been that of a magistrate before whom they were brought for breaches of the peace while on shore leave. He now said : " From what I observed in the behaviour of the sailors in this voyage . . . I am convinced . . . that in their own element, there are no persons near the level of their degree who live in the constant practice of half so many good qualities. . . . All these, however, they always leave behind them on ship-board ; the sailor out of water is, indeed, as wretched an animal as the fish out of water ; for though the former hath, in common with amphibious animals, the bare power of existing on land, yet if he be kept there any time, he never fails to become a nuisance."

The scandalous jobbery of the navy and the consequent ignoring of men who had really earned promotion, aroused his ready indignation. One stormy day when the women had been driven to their bunks, Captain Veal told Fielding something of his past experience, and " informed me " he says " of such misadventures that had befallen him within forty-six years at sea, as might frighten a very bold spirit from undertaking even the smallest voyage. Were these indeed but universally known," Fielding adds, " our matrons of quality would possibly be deterred from venturing their tender offspring at sea ; by which means our navy would lose the honour of many a young commodore who, at twenty-two, is better versed in maritime affairs than real seamen are made by experience at sixty."

The magistrate's eye was not blind to the goings-on of

the Portuguese pilot who evaded the strict quarantine regulations which forbade any passengers landing in a Portuguese port until the boat had been examined by the authorities. This pilot, " for a very small reward," rowed a priest on shore before the examination had taken place, and while the *Queen of Portugal* was waiting on the tide outside the harbour. The pilot did not dare to land his passenger nearer the port, and Fielding remarks that in venturing so far, " he had given sufficient testimony of love for his native country."

When he had said goodbye to his children, it was with the conviction that he should not see them again, and many times during the journal of the voyage he writes as if in the calm acceptance of death: "This work, if I should live to finish it, a matter of no great certainty, if indeed of any great hope to me—" and it is this which gives particular poignancy to his account, unsentimental and filled with ardent, single-minded admiration, of the sunset off Cape Finisterre. "We were seated on the deck, women and all, in the serenest evening that can be imagined ; not a single cloud presented itself to our view, and the sun himself was the only object which engrossed our whole attention. He did indeed set with a majesty which is incapable of description, with which, while the horizon was yet blazing with glory, our eyes were called off to the opposite part, to survey the moon, which was then at full, and which in rising, presented us with the second object which this world hath offered to our vision. Compared to these, the pageantry of theatres or splendour of courts, are sights almost below the regard of children."

The conclusion of the journey is in character with all the rest. His sympathetic pleasure in the delight the women took in the moon-shiny night, his ironic unresentful

recollection of the magistrate of health who visited the ship
to inspect the passengers. Since this dignitary had to visit
the cabin in any case, Captain Veal asked whether the sick,
helpless man might remain below for his examination, instead
of being hoisted on deck ; but this did not satisfy the magistrate's strict regard to his duty, and he called out with a voice
of authority : " Let him be brought up." The party got
off at seven in the evening, and after a drive " through the
nastiest city in the world, though at the same time one of the
most populous," they came to where their dinner had been
ordered, in " a kind of coffee house, very pleasantly situated
on the brow of a hill, about a mile from the city," with " a
very fine prospect of the River Tago from Lisbon to the
sea." Here the party sat down to a good supper, for which
they were charged as much " as if the bill had been made
on the Bath road between Newbury and London." So we
see the last of him, at his cheerful meal in the evening light ;
his surroundings a foreign city, but his mind returning to
England, and the great roads of the West.

Hic finis chartæque viæque, are the last words of the journal.
He died less than three months later, on October 8, 1754.

With what delight, with what pain, with what admiration and love, we read his final work. Fielding has little
in him of the poet and less of the mystic, but in the great
qualities he has he enlarges our conception of the human
kind. We think of him not only as a great novelist, though
he is among the greatest, or as a great magistrate with every
attribute which that implies, though no one ever deserved
the title more, but above all as a great human being :

> the elements
> So mixed in him, that Nature might stand up
> And say to all the world, This was a Man !

BIBLIOGRAPHY

AUSTIN DOBSON. *Fielding*. English Men of Letters Series.

GODDEN, G. M. *Henry Fielding, A Memoir*.

JONES, C. B. *Fielding, Novelist and Magistrate*.

MURPHY, ARTHUR. *The Works of Henry Fielding, Esq., with an Essay on his Life and Genius*.

WORTLEY MONTAGU, LADY MARY. *Letters*.